Francis Frith's
Brighton & Hove

Photographic Memories

Francis Frith's
Brighton & Hove

Revised edition of original work by

Helen Livingston

FRITH
BOOK Co

Revised paperback edition published in the United Kingdom in 2000 by
Frith Book Company Ltd

First published in the United Kingdom in 1998
by WBC Ltd

British Library Cataloguing in Publication Data

Francis Frith's Brighton & Hove
Helen Livingston
ISBN 1-85937-192-2

Frith Book Company Ltd
Frith's Barn, Teffont,
Salisbury, Wiltshire SP3 5QP
Tel: +44 (0) 1722 716 376
Email: info@frithbook.co.uk
www.frithbook.co.uk

Printed and bound in Great Britain

Front Cover: The Beach 1898 41890

Contents

Francis Frith: *Victorian Pioneer*

FRANCIS FRITH, Victorian founder of the world-famous photographic archive, was a complex and multitudinous man. A devout Quaker and a highly successful Victorian businessman, he was both philosophic by nature and pioneering in outlook.

By 1855 Francis Frith had already established a wholesale grocery business in Liverpool, and sold it for the astonishing sum of £200,000, which is the equivalent today of over £15,000,000. Now a multi-millionaire, he was able to indulge his passion for travel. As a child he had pored over travel books written by early explorers, and his fancy and imagination had been stirred by family holidays to the sublime mountain regions of Wales and Scotland. 'What a land of spirit-stirring and enriching scenes and places!' he had written. He was to return to these scenes of grandeur in later years to 'recapture the thousands of vivid and tender memories', but with a different purpose. Now in his thirties, and captivated by the new science of photography, Frith set out on a series of pioneering journeys to the Nile regions that occupied him from 1856 until 1860.

Intrigue and Adventure

He took with him on his travels a specially-designed wicker carriage that acted as both dark-room and sleeping chamber. These far-flung journeys were packed with intrigue and adventure. In his life story, written when he was sixty-three, Frith tells of being held captive by bandits, and of fighting 'an awful midnight battle to the very point of surrender with a deadly pack of hungry, wild dogs'. Sporting flowing Arab costume, Frith arrived at Akaba by camel seventy years before Lawrence, where he encountered 'desert princes and rival sheikhs, blazing with jewel-hilted swords'.

During these extraordinary adventures he was assiduously exploring the desert regions bordering the Nile and patiently recording the antiquities and peoples with his camera. He was the first photographer to venture beyond the sixth cataract. Africa was still the mysterious 'Dark Continent', and Stanley and Livingstone's historic meeting was a decade into the future. The conditions for picture taking confound belief. He laboured for hours in his wicker dark-room in the sweltering heat of the desert, while the volatile chemicals fizzed dangerously in their trays. Often he was forced to work in remote tombs and caves where conditions were cooler. Back in London he exhibited his photographs and was 'rapturously cheered' by members of the Royal Society. His reputation as a photographer was made overnight. An eminent modern historian has likened their impact on the population of the time to that on our own generation of the first photographs taken on the surface of the moon.

Venture of a Life-Time

Characteristically, Frith quickly spotted the opportunity to create a new business as a specialist publisher of photographs. He lived in an era of immense and sometimes violent change. For the poor in the early part of Victoria's reign work was a drudge and the hours long, and people had precious little free time to enjoy themselves. Most had no transport other than a cart or gig at their disposal, and had not travelled far beyond the

boundaries of their own town or village. However, by the 1870s, the railways had threaded their way across the country, and Bank Holidays and half-day Saturdays had been made obligatory by Act of Parliament. All of a sudden the ordinary working man and his family were able to enjoy days out and see a little more of the world.

With characteristic business acumen, Francis Frith foresaw that these new tourists would enjoy having souvenirs to commemorate their days out. In 1860 he married Mary Ann Rosling and set out with the intention of photographing every city, town and village in Britain. For the next thirty years he travelled the country by train and by pony and trap, producing fine photographs of seaside resorts and beauty spots that were keenly bought by millions of Victorians. These prints were painstakingly pasted into family albums and pored over during the dark nights of winter, rekindling precious memories of summer excursions.

The Rise of Frith & Co

Frith's studio was soon supplying retail shops all over the country. To meet the demand he gathered about him a small team of photographers, and published the work of independent artist-photographers of the calibre of Roger Fenton and Francis Bedford. In order to gain some understanding of the scale of Frith's business one only has to look at the catalogue issued by Frith & Co in 1886: it runs to some 670 pages, listing not only many thousands of views of the British Isles but also many photographs of most European countries, and China, Japan, the USA and

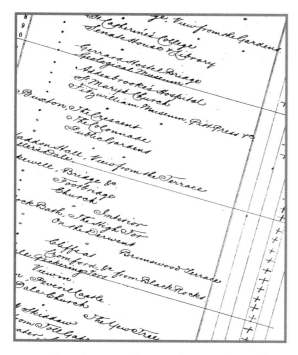

Canada – note the sample page shown above from the hand-written *Frith & Co* ledgers detailing pictures taken. By 1890 Frith had created the greatest specialist photographic publishing company in the world, with over 2,000 outlets – more than the combined number that Boots and WH Smith have today! The picture on the right shows the *Frith & Co* display board at Ingleton in the Yorkshire Dales. Beautifully constructed with mahogany frame and gilt inserts, it could display up to a dozen local scenes.

Postcard Bonanza

The ever-popular holiday postcard we know today took many years to develop. In 1870 the Post Office issued the first plain cards, with a pre-printed stamp on one face. In 1894 they allowed other publishers' cards to be sent through the mail with an attached adhesive halfpenny stamp. Demand grew rapidly, and in 1895 a new size of postcard was permitted called the court card, but there was little room for illustration. In 1899, a year after Frith's death, a new card measuring 5.5 x 3.5 inches became the standard format, but it was not until 1902 that the divided back came into being, with address and message on one face and a full-size illustration on the other. *Frith & Co* were in the vanguard of postcard development, and Frith's sons Eustace and Cyril continued their father's monumental task, expanding the number of views offered to the public and recording more and more places in Britain, as the coasts and countryside were opened up to mass travel.

Francis Frith died in 1898 at his villa in Cannes, his great project still growing. The archive he created continued in business for another seventy years. By 1970 it contained over a third of a million pictures of 7,000 cities, towns and villages. The massive photographic record Frith has left to us stands as a living monument to a special and very remarkable man.

Frith's Archive: *A Unique Legacy*

FRANCIS FRITH'S legacy to us today is of immense significance and value, for the magnificent archive of evocative photographs he created provides a unique record of change in 7,000 cities, towns and villages throughout Britain over a century and more. Frith and his fellow studio photographers revisited locations many times down the years to update their views, compiling for us an enthralling and colourful pageant of British life and character.

We tend to think of Frith's sepia views of Britain as nostalgic, for most of us use them to conjure up memories of places in our own lives with which we have family associations. It often makes us forget that to Francis Frith they were records of daily life as it was actually being lived in the cities, towns and villages of his day. The Victorian age was one of great and often bewildering change for ordinary people, and though the pictures evoke an impression of slower times, life was as busy and hectic as it is today.

We are fortunate that Frith was a photographer of the people, dedicated to recording the minutiae of everyday life. For it is this sheer wealth of visual data, the painstaking chronicle of changes in dress, transport, street layouts, buildings, housing, engineering and landscape that captivates us so much today. His remarkable images offer us a powerful link with the past and with the lives of our ancestors.

Today's Technology

Computers have now made it possible for Frith's many thousands of images to be accessed almost instantly. In the Frith archive today, each photograph is carefully 'digitised' then stored on a CD Rom. Frith archivists can locate a single photograph amongst thousands within seconds. Views can be catalogued and sorted under a variety of categories of place and content to the immediate benefit of researchers.

Inexpensive reference prints can be created for them at the touch of a mouse button, and a wide range of books and other printed materials assembled and published for a wider, more general readership - in the next twelve months over a hundred Frith local history titles will be published! The day-to-day workings of the archive are very different from how they were in Francis Frith's time: imagine the herculean task of sorting through eleven tons of glass negatives as Frith had to do to locate a particular

See Frith at www. frithbook.co.uk

sequence of pictures! Yet the archive still prides itself on maintaining the same high standards of excellence laid down by Francis Frith, including the painstaking cataloguing and indexing of every view.

It is curious to reflect on how the internet now allows researchers in America and elsewhere greater instant access to the archive than Frith himself ever enjoyed. Many thousands of individual views can be called up on screen within seconds on one of the Frith internet sites, enabling people living continents away to revisit the streets of their ancestral home town, or view places in Britain where they have enjoyed holidays. Many overseas researchers welcome the chance to view special theme selections, such as transport, sports, costume and ancient monuments.

We are certain that Francis Frith would have heartily approved of these modern developments in imaging techniques, for he himself was always working at the very limits of Victorian photographic technology.

The Value of the Archive Today

Because of the benefits brought by the computer, Frith's images are increasingly studied by social historians, by researchers into genealogy and ancestory, by architects, town planners, and by teachers and schoolchildren involved in local history projects.

In addition, the archive offers every one of us an opportunity to examine the places where we and our families have lived and worked down the years. Highly successful in Frith's own era, the archive is now, a century and more on, entering a new phase of popularity.

The Past in Tune with the Future

Historians consider the Francis Frith Collection to be of prime national importance. It is the only archive of its kind remaining in private ownership and has been valued at a million pounds. However, this figure is now rapidly increasing as digital technology enables more and more people around the world to enjoy its benefits.

Francis Frith's archive is now housed in an historic timber barn in the beautiful village of Teffont in Wiltshire. Its founder would not recognize the archive office as it is today. In place of the many thousands of dusty boxes containing glass plate negatives and an all-pervading odour of photographic chemicals, there are now ranks of computer screens. He would be amazed to watch his images travelling round the world at unimaginable speeds through network and internet lines.

The archive's future is both bright and exciting. Francis Frith, with his unshakeable belief in making photographs available to the greatest number of people, would undoubtedly approve of what is being done today with his lifetime's work. His photographs, depicting our shared past, are now bringing pleasure and enlightenment to millions around the world a century and more after his death.

Palace Pier 1902 48513
The Palace Pier opened in 1899. This view shows
the recently completed oriental pier head pavilion -
the Marine Pavilion.

The Piers

A walk to the end of the pier has been an essential ingredient in a Brighton holiday since the Chain Pier opened in 1823. The pier was designed as a landing stage for the cross-channel trade (Brighton to Dieppe was on the quickest route between London and Paris), but it was immediately popular with 'promenaders', who paid 2d, or one guinea annually, to walk the 13 ft wide, 1,154 ft long wooden deck. Brighton's Chain Pier was the first pleasure pier ever built, with kiosks contained in its towers and other attractions, including a camera obscura, at the shore end. The pier stood just to the east of the present Palace Pier, but today nothing remains. In its day it was a particularly fine structure, and both Constable and Turner were inspired to paint it. The entrance was via a new esplanade along the foot of the cliff, where the Aquarium (now the Sea Life Centre) now stands. The Chain Pier's popularity then took a tumble; in 1891, the Marine Palace and Pier Company was given permission to build a new pier (the Palace Pier), on condition that they demolished the Chain Pier. The company did not have to fulfil this condition - it was completely destroyed in a storm on 4 December 1896.

The West Pier, by the famous pier designer Eugenius Birch, opened in 1866, providing a fashionable promenade pier for the western side of Brighton. Initially there were few buildings on the pier, but in 1893 the pier head was widened and a large pavilion built. This was converted to a theatre in 1903 (it had its own repertory company during the 1930s) but in 1945 it was turned into an amusement arcade. A concert hall was added in the centre in 1916. Day ▶

trips to France from the West Pier were popular during the inter-war years.

The Palace Pier opened in 1899 and was straightaway a huge success. In 1901 it was embellished with a landing stage and an oriental-style pier head pavilion. The pavilion was remodelled as a theatre in 1910-11 at the same time as the bandstand (now the cafes) and the Winter Garden (now the Palace of Fun) were added. The theatre was demolished in 1974 after severe damage by a barge associated with the demolition of the landing stage. Pier head slot machines and funfair rides took its place. The Palace Pier has always been extremely popular, rising to its apex in 1939 when 2 million people visited it; 45,000 visited in just one bank holiday.

▼ **Palace Pier 1902** 48509
This view of he Palace Pier was taken from the sea, showing the elegant Brighton seafront and several pleasure craft.

◄ **Palace Pier c1955** B208022
This busy summer scene looking east shows the remodelled entrance to the Palace Pier and the eastern beaches.

▲ **The Chain Pier c1880**
B2085017
This view of the Chain Pier from the west shows the pier head, designed as a landing stage for cross-channel traffic.

◀ **Looking East from the Pier c1955** B208103
We are looking east from the Palace Pier towards Black Rock, an area now dominated by the concrete breakwater of the Brighton Marina.

▼ **Palace Pier c1960** B208112
This view of the Palace Pier from Marine Parade shows how it had developed since 1902, with the addition of an entrance, clocktower and winter gardens.

▼ **West Pier c1880** B2085018
The historic West Pier was opened in 1866. This view shows the Pier before its extensive additions from 1890 onwards.

▲ **The Pier 1889** 22345
This view shows a still undeveloped West Pier. Beached boats are a reminder of Brighton's days as a fishing village.

◄ West Pier from King's Road 1894 33762
This view shows the West Pier, its landing stage and paddle steamers. Benches are visible on the beach - the forerunners of deckchairs.

◄ **West Pier 1894** 33718
Here we see another
view of the West Pier,
this time looking from
the east, with horse-
drawn conveyances
waiting for custom.

◄ **West Pier 1894** 33717
Here we see the West Pier during the 'fashionable' autumnal season, sporting its new pier head pavilion and landing stage.

▼ **The Pier c1896**
B2085009
The 1896 storm that destroyed the Chain Pier badly damaged the West Pier, as this picture shows, and the partly-built Palace Pier.

◄ **West Pier 1902** 48493
It is a glorious summer's day; this is the West Pier beach, busy with holiday makers, bathing machines and boats.

▼ **West Pier 1902** 48494

This view shows the front of the 1,115 ft West Pier, showing clearly the two toll booths - only the left booth now survives.

▼ **The Ferry 1902** 48508

There was a thriving trade in excursions along the coast and to France. This view shows a ferry, probably the 'Brighton Queen', leaving the West Pier.

▲ **West Pier 1902** 48497

We are looking back to the shore from the West Pier. The delicate wrought-iron features of this Victorian masterpiece are clearly visible.

◄ **West Pier 1921** 71495
This view of the West Pier
shows it in its final form,
with the central Concert Hall
built in 1916.

West Pier 1902 48495
Here we see another
view of the West Pier.
Note the fishing boats
out at sea beyond the
left-hand toll booth.

◀ **From the Pier 1921**
71486
This view taken from the
pier shows many
changes since 1902: the
Concert Hall, the
lifeboats and the
fashions.

◄ West Pier 1921 71496
This is another view of the West Pier, showing clearly its completed buildings. Deckchairs are lined up on the Kings Road Promenade.

▼ View from West Pier c1955 B208015
This view of the West Pier looks towards King's Road and the Metropole Hotel.

◄ The Boating Lake 1925 78309
This picture shows the boating lake. Between the wars, the pier was used for day trips to France, and had its own Customs officials.

Rottingdean, The Undercliff Walk c1965 R62082
A picture postcard view of Rottingdean seafront, looking west towards Brighton and Worthing.

**Rottingdean,
The Cliffs and the Swimming Pool c1965** R62065
The Rottingdean sea water baths opened in 1935, and enjoyed a superb location beneath the cliffs. They closed in 1990.

The Seafront
Rottingdean to the Palace Pier

The steep-cliffed nature of Brighton's eastern seafront from Rottingdean to the Palace Pier gives it quite a different flavour to the seafront to the west. The beach lies well below the main clifftop road, and was originally the ladies' bathing beach. Ladies would enter the water from bathing machines licensed by Brighton Corporation. They cost 9d per half hour (6d for gentlemen). There were 150 ladies' machines and 100 gentlemen's in 1880. Mixed bathing was finally sanctioned by the corporation in 1901 - and then only from bathing machines. Seventy-nine years later the world was changed indeed, with Brighton as the first major resort to sanction a naturist beach - at Cliff bathing beach below Duke's Mound.

East Brighton's seafront architecture is of the highest standard. It developed eastwards from the Steine from the 1790s, and reached Kemp Town in the 1850s; there are a succession of inspiring terraces and villas, including Eastern Terrace and Royal Crescent, as well as the fine Grade 1 listed Kemp Town estate itself. During the 'Fashionable Season' between October and January, the rich and famous would 'promenade' by the sea and on the pier in the mornings, and then spend the afternoon driving along the seafront drives of Marine Parade and King's Road from Kemp Town to Brunswick Town.

In order to protect the prestigious dwellings of Marine Parade, a great sea wall was built along the cliff in the 1830s, and a road was constructed along it. This was immediately fashionable with 'promenaders' because of its sheltered location and its proximity to the Chain Pier. It was rebuilt as Madeira Drive (known as Madeira Road until the First World War), and improved in the 1890s with the building of Madeira Terrace raised on its graceful cast iron arches; the Madeira Lift carried people from Madeira Drive to Marine Parade. Madeira Drive has always been popular for events like the National Speed Trials.

The Undercliff walk from Black Rock to Rottingdean opened in 1933, part of a scheme to protect the cliffed coast. The extension to Saltdean opened in 1935, at the same time as the opening of Rottingdean swimming pool in its superb location at the foot of the cliffs. The open-air pool at Black Rock opened in 1936. Both pools have now closed, and the Undercliff at Black Rock is dominated by the Marina.

Other attractions of the eastern seafront included the Chain Pier of 1823, the Aquarium which opened in 1872, and Volk's Electric Railway, opened in 1883, the first such railway, which still runs along the shore between the beach and Madeira Drive.

◄ **Marine Parade 1921**
71499
This view looks westwards from Marine Parade, showing the handsome Regency seafront and buses parked along Madeira Drive.

◄ Madeira Road 1902

48517

This view looks westwards along Madeira Terrace towards the piers. Promenaders stroll in the sun, and a horse-drawn vehicle drives along Madeira Drive.

▼ Eastern Terrace c1955

B208069

This is a view of the imposing Eastern Terrace, nine four-storied houses on Marine Parade, which date from the 1830s.

◄ The Promenade c1955

B208503

It is a hot summer's day. On the left is the Palace Pier entrance, whilst on the right is the Aquarium and terrace.

◀ **Marine Parade c1955**
B208019
From close to the
entrance to the Palace
Pier, we are looking East
along Marine Parade.
Note the lack of road
markings.

◄ The Seafront c1955
B208071
This view was taken from the top of the Aquarium sun terrace. Coaches are parked along Madeira Drive.

▼ The Aquarium 1921
71498
Here we see the Aquarium Clock Tower and entrance. By the end of the decade, this frontage was swept away.

◄ The Aquarium and the Promenade c1955
B208504
We are looking east along the front to the Aquarium and Marine Drive, here thronged with holiday makers.

◀ **The Aquarium c1955**
B208502
This view shows the
remodelled Aquarium,
with its two square
kiosks and pagoda roofs.

◄ **The Aquarium 1889**
22238
This view shows the entrance to the Aquarium, which opened in 1872. Goat carts awaiting customers are visible on the left of the picture.

▼ **The Promenade c1955**
B208097
This is a bustling view of the promenade by the Aquarium entrance. The occupants of the deckchairs are clearly enjoying their rest.

◄ **From Palace Pier 1902** 48515
This is an early view from the Palace Pier, looking to the West Pier. The Union Jack flutters proudly from one of the many hotels.

◄ **The Beach c1955**
B208096
We are looking
eastwards from the
Palace Pier along the
seafront to the cliffs at
Rottingdean.

◄ **From Palace Pier 1902** 48514
Bathing machines vie for space with fishing boats on the 'gentlemen's beach'.

▼ **The Front c1955**
B208116
We are looking west from Palace Pier. Bathing machines and boats have vanished from the beach.

◄ **The Front c1955**
B208115
Here we see the handsome skyline presented by Brighton to the seas as seen from the Palace Pier.

**From Palace Pier
1902** 48514A
This view looks west
from the Palace Pier.
Bathing machines can
be seen drawn up at the
top of the beach.

The Beach 1898 41890
In this jostling view of Brighton Beach, holidaymakers, entertainers, boats and bathing machines fill the picture. The Palace Pier is still under construction.

The Beach 1902 48503
This is a timeless scene: children playing on the
seafront. Before the invention of deckchairs, the beach
sported wooden benches.

The Seafront
The Palace Pier to King's Esplanade

Busy, breezy 'Doctor Brighton', where the crowds came to take the waters and be dipped in the sea, is epitomised by the pictures of the seafront from the Palace Pier westwards to Hove. King's Road, the seafront road of west Brighton, is named after George I, who opened it in 1822. It was part of the principal 'carriage drive' of the town, and as such was not surfaced with tarmac until 1910. It was widened in the 1850s and 60s, and again in the 1880s, when the King's Road Arches were constructed beneath it and the birdcage bandstand built.

There is notable architecture in West Brighton, although the 20th century has punctuated and interrupted the majestic sweep of Regency and Victorian buildings. Big hotels like The Grand, The Norfolk and The Metropole still face seaward, but modern developments have replaced the old Bedford and the famous Mutton's, which closed in 1929. Regency developments like Brunswick Terrace (Hove) and Regency Square lend their elegance to West Brighton.

The Lower Esplanade from Palace Pier westwards to the lawns of Hove has always been the 'honky tonk' part of Brighton's seafront, the haunt of stalls and entertainers and later of private beach chalets, cafes and amusement arcades. The Western Lawns ▶

beyond the bandstand were laid out in the 1880s; they were improved in 1925 with the addition of a boating pool and putting green, and again for the Festival of Britain in 1953. Beach donkeys were a feature of the Brighton seafront until the Second World War. They plied the lower esplanade with their youthful mounts, since the pebbly beach made it impossible for them to be ridden there. Dark rumours hung around these donkeys in the mid 19th century, for they were reputed to be used clandestinely by the local smuggling fraternity to carry contraband spirits. Goat carts were available for children to hire from the 1830s - they were expensive, costing one shilling per hour by the mid 19th century. The beach was always busy, and beach entertainers, including 'minstrels' with blackened faces, were very popular, though frequently of dubious merit. From 1891, pierrots in their black and white costumes were introduced from France. During the 19th and early 20th centuries there was a great vogue for boat trips from the beach; many former fishing vessels were thus employed, notably the 'Skylark', a boat that became so famous that 'Skylark' became a generic term for the pleasure boats of Brighton.

Kings Road 1902 48492
This Edwardian view of King's Road shows the famous Metropole and Grand Hotels, as well as Bolla & Bucchi's Restaurant in the King's Road Arches on the Lower Esplanade.

◄ **Kings Road 1925**
78308
Only a few years separates this from photograph No 71492, but there has been a further change of ownership of the arches, now reduced to selling ice cream.

◀ Kings Road 1921

71492

Nineteen years after photograph No 48492, the big hotels gaze impassively on a less crowded beach, whilst the New Savoy Arches Restaurant is touting for business on the Lower Esplanade.

▼ The Beach 1902 48502

Nautical Brighton: a steamer arrives at the West Pier, whilst yachts are drawn up on the beach ready for sailing.

◀ The Beach and the Putting Green c1955

B208120

The centrepiece of this scene is the putting green on the Lower Esplanade, constructed in 1935-8. Cafes and amusements are found in the King's Road Arches.

▼ **The Seafront c1955** B208118
Here we see the seafront looking to the West Pier. The ice cream men
are out in force, and a beer lorry delivers to a café.

▼ **From West Pier 1902** 48501
This view looks eastwards from the West Pier to the new Palace Pier.
The big groynes were built to counter coastal erosion.

▲ **The Parade 1921** 71490
The deck chairs have
today made way for a
cycle track, and there is a
paddling pool on the
extreme left. The ramp is
above the site of
Brighton's lifeboat station,
1887-1931.

◄ **The Children's Paddling Pool c1955** B208090
This is a busy and nostalgic scene of the paddling pool by the West Pier. The pool was constructed in 1935-8.

▼ **The Promenade and Kings Road c1955** B208507
This evening view looks towards the ramp from whence
picture No B208090 was taken.

▼ **The Children's Pool c1955** B208013
Another view of the paddling pool looking westwards. Note the private
chalets under the arches.

▲ **The Metropole Hotel
1925** 78312
This view of The
Metropole shows little
change since the
beginning of the century.
The massive proportions
of this red brick hotel
dwarf its more modest
neighbours.

◄ **The Parade 1921** 71491
Here we see a classic view
of Brighton. This evocative
picture of the promenaders
is reminiscent of one of the
most famous Brighton
posters of the interwar
years, entitled 'Brighton:
Fame & Fashion'.

THIS FREEHOLD
TO BE SOLD
Mr RAWLINSON

**The Seafront Hotels
1890** 27609
This view shows two of
Brighton's famous
hotels: on the left is The
Metropole, which
opened that year, the
largest hotel outside
London, and on the
right is The Grand.

▼ **The Children's Boating Pool c1955** B208088
Here we see a happy scene at the children's boating pool, which first
opened in 1925. The building beyond was built for the Festival of
Britain as the Western Bathing Pavilion.

▼ **The Boating Pool c1955** B208124
The boating pool was a favourite spot in the 1950s, and this photo
suggests that it would continue forever. Sadly, it was not to be. It is
now a petanque terrain.

▲ **Kings Road 1902** 48505
A classic Edwardian
scene: elegance, straw
hats and parasols
promenade along the
King's Esplanade, a
fashionable resort at the
height of its fame.

◀ **Kings Road 1890** 27607
A timeless late Victorian scene along the King's Esplanade: in the foreground, mother and father are taking their daughter for a stroll along the terrace.

◄ **Kings Road looking East 1902** 48491
Time moves on, but little has changed in this scene. Horse carriages are visible on King's Road, whilst bathing machines are drawn up on the right.

◄ The Parade 1894

33719

This view from the bandstand shows a donkey on the Lower Esplanade watched by a child on the Parade. The old Bedford Hotel is in the centre of the picture.

▼ Looking Eastward 1921 71488

This view, taken from the same spot as photograph No 48491, shows some changes, with deckchairs ranged along the parade.

◄ The Promenade 1894

33721

This view is looking west from the bandstand to Hove. The low building on the right is the former Brunswick Baths, now replaced by Embassy Court.

◀ **The Seafront 1925**
78303
This view looking towards the Peace Memorial proudly shows the newly created Brunswick Gardens, part of major improvements to the seafront.

◄ **The Seafront 1921**

71489

This view looks west to the Hove boundary and the Peace Memorial, which is actually a memorial to Edward VII.

▼ **The Promenade Gardens c1955** B208506

We are looking from the Hove Boundary to the bandstand, with a closer view of the gardens.

◄ **The Lawns c1955**

B208505

This view looks east across Hove Lawns. The Peace Memorial and the Norfolk Hotel dominate the Brighton-Hove boundary.

◀ **Hove, The Lawns 1921**
71503
Courtenay Terrace is the only group of houses which had gardens backing onto the beach. The built-up prom today extends westwards past the houses, but miraculously they and their gardens survive.

The Promenade 1921

71500

This evocative view echoes the distinctive atmosphere of Hove - the elegant and sophisticated sister of Brighton. The superb Regency skyline provides a fitting setting for walking the baby.

Hove, The Bowling Green c1960   H128011

This gentle scene of Hove bowling green is a world away from bustling, cosmopolitan Brighton. The green is still very much part of the Hove scene.

Hove, The Boating Lake c1960   H128006

The Hove boating lake was a venue for model boat enthusiasts. Today it is used for wind surfing.

◄ **North Street c1955**
B208501
This view of North Street
looks towards the
Countess of
Huntingdon's Chapel.
Hugely popular in its
day, and able to seat
2,000 people, it was
demolished in 1972.

Brighton Town

The Steine c1880

B2085012

A fascinating view across the Steine showing Marlborough House, Steine House and Blenheim House. All three buildings are still standing. The magnificent fountain was built in 1846 for Queen Victoria's 27th birthday.

Old Brighton was a coastal fishing village bounded by West Street, East Street and North Street, that area of town now known as 'the lanes'. There was once a South Street, and indeed a whole 'lower town' on the beach, but they were claimed by the sea in the early 18th century. To the east of East Street, a marshy valley, the Steine (pronounced 'Steen') with a little stream, the Wellesbourne, ran down to the coast. Here fishermen would spread their nets to dry, and here was the farmhouse where the Prince Regent (George IV) stayed. He took a liking to the place, and ended up building the Royal Pavilion, Brighton's best known building, which is now listed Grade 1. Brighton was a 'spa' town before the Prince arrived, thanks to a treatise on the use of sea water by Dr Russell of Lewes, published in 1754. Royal patronage ensured that it became the fashionable place to 'take the waters', and the town developed apace. Up went the Regency terraces, squares and villas for which Brighton is famous, a style of building which continued here well into the Victorian era. The Steine became the place to 'promenade', and various improvements took place with the building of the North and South Parades. In 1823 the Steine was enclosed with tall iron fencing, and the following year it was provided with gas lights.

When the railway arrived in Brighton in 1841 it brought with it a new kind of visitor, the 'tripper'; the town grew greatly in size, filling up with hotels, boarding houses, cafes, restaurants and theatres. North Street and East Street, the principal shopping streets, bustled with activity. Brighton was also famed for its schools, which took advantage of Brighton's reputation as a health-giving place; they found perfect accommodation in large Regency villas.

Brighton's parish church, St Peter's, was built in the 1820s at Richmond Green, just north of the Steine, and designated as the parish church in 1873. It was originally a chapel-of-ease to the old parish church of St Nicholas, set up on the hill to the west; this was the burial place of Brighton worthies like Martha Gunn, the most famous Brighton 'dipper', and Phoebe Hessell, who had disguised herself as a man to fight in the British army alongside her lover. St Peter's was designed by Sir Charles Barry, later the architect of the Houses of Parliament.

◄ **The Pavilion c1955**
B208081
This view of the Pavilion shows off its ornate oriental style to advantage. A Grade 1 listed building, it has been restored in recent years to its original condition.

The Pavilion 1902 ▶
48524

This photograph shows the Dome. It was originally built in 1803-8 as stables for the Pavilion, but was converted to a magnificent concert hall, capable of seating 2,500 people.

◀ **The Pavilion 1889**
22244

Another superb view of the Pavilion, showing clearly its remarkable Indian façade; it was built for the Prince of Wales (George IV) in the early 1800s.

The Pavilion ▶
c1955 B208018

This view shows the main entrance to the Pavilion. It is difficult to imagine how it must have appeared to Brighton's simple fisherfolk.

Victoria Gardens ▶
1898 41901

Although Queen Victoria deserted Brighton for the Isle of Wight, the town celebrated her Diamond Jubilee by opening the Victoria Gardens. This splendid statue forms the centrepiece.

The Old Steine ▶
1902 48522
Note the tall railings and the lack of traffic. The trams began operating the year before, with the Steine as their main terminus.

◀ The Clock Tower
c1942 B2085008
A wartime view of the 75ft high clock tower, built in 1888 to celebrate the Queen's Golden Jubilee a year earlier.

◀ London Road c1880
B2085015
A steam-driven engine and what appears to be a furrowing machine are standing in London Road. They are probably engaged in ripping up the roads to construct the tramways.

◀ **St Peter's Church
1902** 48523
St Peter's, the parish
church of Brighton,
dominates the area just
north of the Steine. It
was built in 1824-8.
Today, it is rather
marooned between the
London and Lewes
roads.

◄ **The Steine c1880**
B2085010
Another fine shot of the tramway construction in the Steine, looking directly to where photograph No B2085002 was taken. The extensive network was completed in 1904, and trams ran until just before the Second World War.

◀ The Steine c1880
B2085002
A turn-of-the-century view of the tramway construction taking place in the Steine. The photographer is looking towards North Road.

▼ The Steine c1880
B2085004
An excellent close-up of the navvies building the tramlines round the Steine. The photographer has caught to perfection the hard labour required.

◀ Lewes Road c1880
B2085001
Tramway construction is going on at the junction of Lewes Road and Elm Grove. The tracks curving away to the right terminated by the racecourse. The view has changed greatly today.

Queen's Road c1880
B2085007
This view shows tram No 22 heading down Queen's Road from the Station. The buildings behind have all been demolished and replaced.

▲ **Rottingdean, the Downs c1955** R62044
Here we see Rottingdean windmill. It was built in 1802, fell into disuse later in the century and was later restored.

◀ **Rottingdean, The School c1965** R62043
The secluded nature of Rottingdean is evident in this view, showing it tucked into a fold of the South Downs.

The Environs of Brighton

▼ **Rottingdean, The Village c1965** R62081
This view shows Rottingdean pond. It was once popular with downland shepherds, but it dried up in 1976 and is now pumped from the well.

Since the early 19th century Brighton has been synonymous with fame and fashion, so perhaps it is only natural that nearby Hove prides itself on its gentility. Hove has developed from a number of hamlets to the west of Brighton. It has ancient roots, but it only started to grow in the 19th century when it began to fall into the gravitational pull of its big sister. The waters of St Anne's Well, a chalybeate spring, were recommended by Dr Russell in his treatise and brought visitors to Hove. Brunswick Terrace, perhaps the most magnificent Regency development in Britain, was completed in 1830, and further seafront terraces and squares followed. It says much that when you stand on the beach near the West Pier, the Hove seafront stands out as totally unspoilt, and little changed from these pictures. Beyond the seafront, Church Street is Hove's main commercial street. Up until 1966, it was dominated by the old Hove Town Hall. Although this has now gone, Church Street retains a discreet and gentle air. Hove has some particularly fine churches. The old parish church of St Andrew's nestles incongruously under the Victorian gasometer, and dates back to medieval times. All Saints, built at the end of the 19th century, is a superbly grand affair. St Leonard's, Aldrington, went up in the 1870s, and St John the Baptist's, which was built in 1852 to serve the Adelaide Crescent ▶

development, adds an elegance with a soaring spire of about 1870.

To the east of Brighton is Rottingdean, a coastal village sheltering in a little combe, and still largely untroubled by the presence of its noisy neighbour. If Hove is Brighton's genteel suburb, Rottingdean is Brighton's country cousin. Since the growth of Brighton, Rottingdean, with its 12th-century church built on Saxon foundations, and its tranquil village pond, has long been a magnet for artists and authors. During the Victorian era many were drawn to its peace and solitude, almost cheek by jowl with Brighton. The most famous were Rudyard Kipling and Sir Edward Burne-Jones. Their houses still stand.

Behind Brighton to the north rise the smooth, rolling South Downs. It was inevitable that Brighton's visitors would turn inland and discover their beauty. The magnet was the Devil's Dyke, one of the highest points on the Downs, which has magnificent views over the Weald. A branch railway put the Dyke on the map, and other strange conveyances - a hair-raising cable car across the Dyke and a funicular railway down the scarp slope of the Downs - added to its attractions. All have long since closed.

▼ **Rottingdean, The Street 1896** 37140
The photographer has the undivided attention of a group of children.

◄ **Rottingdean, The Village 1896** 37139
The village looks threadbare by comparison with its manicured look today, reflecting its steady gentrification.

▼ **Rottingdean, The Village c1965** R62087
This picture is taken from a similar position to photograph No 37140. The roof line has changed little, but shops now front the street, which is busy with cars.

▼ **Rottingdean, High Street c1965** R62075
This view shows the road linking the cliffs and shore with the coast road. Thirty years or so later, this view is little altered.

◄ **Rottingdean, The School 1896** 37143
Many schools were established in the Brighton area, for the bracing air was ideal for children. Perhaps the most famous is Roedean, established in new buildings on the clifftop a few years after this picture was taken.

◀ **Rottingdean, The Village c1965**

R62089

A view of The Street, looking south. Again the view has not changed substantially in the past 30 years, but the road has become busier.

▼ **Rottingdean, The Church 1889**

22255

St Margaret's Church dates from the 12th century, but stands on the site of a Saxon church.

◀ **Rottingdean, The Church c1965**

R62048

The church is pleasantly situated by the green; the lychgate was added in 1897.

◀ **Rottingdean, Tudor Close House c1955**

R62020

Tudor Close House was a skilful 1920s conversion of much older farm buildings into seven houses. They were converted into a hotel, as seen in this view, but shortly afterwards the building was reconverted back to twenty-nine flats.

Rottingdean, The Village c1960 R62078
Part of these cottages date back to Tudor times, but otherwise they are a 1930s redevelopment.

Municipal Camping Ground c1955 B208048
This wonderful view shows Brighton's municipal camping ground, the first in the country, which was opened in May 1938.

Municipal Camping Ground c1955 B208058
Another view of the camping ground, showing the former farm buildings on the left. The racecourse on the top of the hill shows just how close the camping ground was to Brighton.

◀ **Hove, Victoria Statue 1902** 48507
Hove's Victoria Statue stands at the south end of Grand Avenue, at one time the most prestigious street in Hove.

◄ Municipal Camping Ground c1955 B208511
The camping ground was situated in the Sheepcote valley, between the racecourse and Black Rock. It incorporated the former Newhouse Farm. It closed in the early 1990s.

▼ Hove, The Town Hall 1898 41894
Here we see a close up of the handsome Town Hall. The Hall was only 16 years old at the time of this photograph. It is sad that it was ravaged by fire in the 1960s and demolished.

◄ Hove, Kingsway Road c1955 H128002
This view shows Kingsway and the parade of shops. Little has changed today, although the Post Office sign on the side of Brown's shop has disappeared.

Hove, The Drive 1898
41895
This splendid view is substantially the same today, although the trees have grown considerably.

◄ **Hove, Kingsway c1955**
H128005
We are looking eastwards down Kingsway. This view has not changed greatly: the pub is still open for trade, although the road has acquired traffic islands.

Hove, Church Road
1898 41896
A bustling scene. This view is dominated by the old Town Hall. In the background can be seen the gasometer.

▼ Hove, The Congregational Church 1898 41898

◄ Hove, Derek Avenue
c1955 H128004
Today, the trees have matured, and the road is now lined with cars.

◄ Hove, St John's Church 1898 41897
St John the Baptist's church stands in Palmeira Square, Hove. This elegant church was built in 1852 to serve the Adelaide Crescent development.

▼ Hove, St Leonard's Church c1960
H128008
This is another study of one of Hove's excellent churches, this time St Leonard's. The church, and its lychgate, are little changed today.

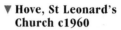

▲ Rottingdean, From the Windmill c1965 R62037
Legend has it that this famous smock mill was used by smugglers for signalling.

◀ **The Devil's Dyke 1894**
33765
A view from the top of
Devil's Dyke, looking north
to the Weald. The church
and village of Poynings are
in the foreground.

The Devil's Dyke 1902 48527

We are looking directly towards the Dyke. To the left of the flagpole can be seen a pier of the Dyke cable car, which stretched across the valley. This vertigo-inducing ride lasted from 1894 to 1907. The places where the piers stood are still visible.

The Devil's Dyke c1955 B208509

This view shows the road over the downs from Poynings to Brighton, with the road to the left heading up to Devil's Dyke. At the bottom of the road is the hamlet of Saddlescombe, now owned by the National Trust.

Index

Frith Book Co Titles

Frith Book Company publish over a 100 new titles each year. For latest catalogue please contact Frith Book Co.

Town Books 96pp, 100 photos. County and Themed Books 128pp, 150 photos
(unless specified) All titles hardback laminated case and jacket
except those indicated pb (paperback)

Around Barnstaple	1-85937-084-5	£12.99
Around Blackpool	1-85937-049-7	£12.99
Around Bognor Regis	1-85937-055-1	£12.99
Around Bristol	1-85937-050-0	£12.99
Around Cambridge	1-85937-092-6	£12.99
Cheshire	1-85937-045-4	£14.99
Around Chester	1-85937-090-X	£12.99
Around Chesterfield	1-85937-071-3	£12.99
Around Chichester	1-85937-089-6	£12.99
Cornwall	1-85937-054-3	£14.99
Cotswolds	1-85937-099-3	£14.99
Around Derby	1-85937-046-2	£12.99
Devon	1-85937-052-7	£14.99
Dorset	1-85937-075-6	£14.99
Dorset Coast	1-85937-062-4	£14.99
Around Dublin	1-85937-058-6	£12.99
East Anglia	1-85937-059-4	£14.99
Around Eastbourne	1-85937-061-6	£12.99
English Castles	1-85937-078-0	£14.99
Around Falmouth	1-85937-066-7	£12.99
Hampshire	1-85937-064-0	£14.99
Isle of Man	1-85937-065-9	£14.99
Around Maidstone	1-85937-056-X	£12.99
North Yorkshire	1-85937-048-9	£14.99
Around Nottingham	1-85937-060-8	£12.99
Around Penzance	1-85937-069-1	£12.99
Around Reading	1-85937-087-X	£12.99
Around St Ives	1-85937-068-3	£12.99
Around Salisbury	1-85937-091-8	£12.99
Around Scarborough	1-85937-104-3	£12.99
Scottish Castles	1-85937-077-2	£14.99
Around Sevenoaks and Tonbridge	1-85937-057-8	£12.99

Sheffield and S Yorkshire	1-85937-070-5	£14.99
Shropshire	1-85937-083-7	£14.99
Staffordshire	1-85937-047-0 (96pp)	£12.99
Suffolk	1-85937-074-8	£14.99
Surrey	1-85937-081-0	£14.99
Around Torbay	1-85937-063-2	£12.99
Wiltshire	1-85937-053-5	£14.99
Around Bakewell	1-85937-113-2	£12.99
Around Bournemouth	1-85937-067-5	£12.99
Cambridgeshire	1-85937-086-1	£14.99
Essex	1-85937-082-9	£14.99
Around Great Yarmouth	1-85937-085-3	£12.99
Hertfordshire	1-85937-079-9	£14.99
Isle of Wight	1-85937-114-0	£14.99
Around Lincoln	1-85937-111-6	£12.99
Oxfordshire	1-85937-076-4	£14.99
Around Shrewsbury	1-85937-110-8	£12.99
South Devon Coast	1-85937-107-8	£14.99
Around Stratford upon Avon	1-85937-098-5	£12.99
West Midlands	1-85937-109-4	£14.99

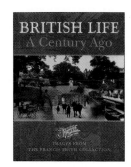

British Life A Century Ago
246 x 189mm
144pp, hardback.
Black and white
Lavishly illustrated with photos
from the turn of the century,
and with extensive commentary.
It offers a unique insight into
the social history and heritage
of bygone Britain.

1-85937-103-5 £17.99

Available from your local bookshop or from the publisher

Around Bath	1-85937-097-7	£12.99	Mar
Cumbria	1-85937-101-9	£14.99	Mar
Down the Thames	1-85937-121-3	£14.99	Mar
Around Exeter	1-85937-126-4	£12.99	Mar
Greater Manchester	1-85937-108-6	£14.99	Mar
Around Harrogate	1-85937-112-4	£12.99	Mar
Around Leicester	1-85937-073-x	£12.99	Mar
Around Liverpool	1-85937-051-9	£12.99	Mar
Northumberland and Tyne & Wear			
	1-85937-072-1	£14.99	Mar
Around Oxford	1-85937-096-9	£12.99	Mar
Around Plymouth	1-85937-119-1	£12.99	Mar
Around Southport	1-85937-106-x	£12.99	Mar
Welsh Castles	1-85937-120-5	£14.99	Mar
Canals and Waterways	1-85937-129-9	£17.99	Apr
Around Guildford	1-85937-117-5	£12.99	Apr
Around Horsham	1-85937-127-2	£12.99	Apr
Around Ipswich	1-85937-133-7	£12.99	Apr
Ireland (pb)	1-85937-181-7	£9.99	Apr
London (pb)	1-85937-183-3	£9.99	Apr
New Forest	1-85937-128-0	£14.99	Apr
Around Newark	1-85937-105-1	£12.99	Apr
Around Newquay	1-85937-140-x	£12.99	Apr
Scotland (pb)	1-85937-182-5	£9.99	Apr
Around Southampton	1-85937-088-8	£12.99	Apr
Sussex (pb)	1-85937-184-1	£9.99	Apr
Around Winchester	1-85937-139-6	£12.99	Apr
Around Belfast	1-85937-094-2	£12.99	May
Colchester (pb)	1-85937-188-4	£8.99	May
Exmoor	1-85937-132-9	£14.99	May
Leicestershire (pb)	1-85937-185-x	£9.99	May
Lincolnshire	1-85937-135-3	£14.99	May
North Devon Coast	1-85937-146-9	£14.99	May
Nottinghamshire (pb)	1-85937-187-6	£9.99	May
Peak District	1-85937-100-0	£14.99	May
Around Truro	1-85937-147-7	£12.99	May
Yorkshire (pb)	1-85937-186-8	£9.99	May

Berkshire (pb)	1-85937-191-4	£9.99	Jun
Brighton (pb)	1-85937-192-2	£8.99	Jun
County Durham	1-85937-123-x	£14.99	Jun
Dartmoor	1-85937-145-0	£14.99	Jun
Down the Severn	1-85937-118-3	£14.99	Jun
East London	1-85937-080-2	£14.99	Jun
East Sussex	1-85937-130-2	£14.99	Jun
Glasgow (pb)	1-85937-190-6	£8.99	Jun
Kent (pb)	1-85937-189-2	£9.99	Jun
Kent Living Memories	1-85937-125-6	£14.99	Jun
Redhill to Reigate	1-85937-137-x	£12.99	Jun
Stone Circles & Ancient Monuments			
	1-85937-143-4	£17.99	Jun
Victorian & Edwardian Kent			
	1-85937-149-3	£14.99	Jun
Victorian & Edwardian Maritime Album			
	1-85937-144-2	£17.99	Jun
Victorian & Edwardian Yorkshire			
	1-85937-154-x	£14.99	Jun
West Sussex	1-85937-148-5	£14.99	Jun
Churches of Berkshire	1-85937-170-1	£17.99	Jul
Churches of Dorset	1-85937-172-8	£17.99	Jul
Derbyshire (pb)	1-85937-196-5	£9.99	Jul
Edinburgh (pb)	1-85937-193-0	£8.99	Jul
Folkstone	1-85937-124-8	£12.99	Jul
Gloucestershire	1-85937-102-7	£14.99	Jul
Herefordshire	1-85937-174-4	£14.99	Jul
North London	1-85937-206-6	£14.99	Jul
Norwich (pb)	1-85937-194-9	£8.99	Jul
Ports and Harbours	1-85937-208-2	£17.99	Jul
Somerset and Avon	1-85937-153-1	£14.99	Jul
South Devon Living Memories			
	1-85937-168-x	£14.99	Jul
Warwickshire (pb)	1-85937-203-1	£9.99	Jul
Worcestershire	1-85937-152-3	£14.99	Jul
Yorkshire Living Memories			
	1-85937-166-3	£14.99	Jul

FRITH PRODUCTS & SERVICES

Francis Frith would doubtless be pleased to know that the pioneering publishing venture he started in 1860 still continues today. More than a hundred and thirty years later, The Francis Frith Collection continues in the same innovative tradition and is now one of the foremost publishers of vintage photographs in the world. Some of the current activities include:

Interior Decoration

Today Frith's photographs can be seen framed and as giant wall murals in thousands of pubs, restaurants, hotels, banks, retail stores and other public buildings throughout the country. In every case they enhance the unique local atmosphere of the places they depict and provide reminders of gentler days in an increasingly busy and frenetic world.

Product Promotions

Frith products have been used by many major companies to promote the sales of their own products or to reinforce their own history and heritage. Brands include Hovis bread, Courage beers, Scots Porage Oats, Colman's mustard, Cadbury's foods, Mellow Birds coffee, Dunhill pipe tobacco, Guinness, and Bulmer's Cider.

Genealogy and Family History

As the interest in family history and roots grows world-wide, more and more people are turning to Frith's photographs of Great Britain for images of the towns, villages and streets where their ancestors lived; and, of course, photographs of the churches and chapels where their ancestors were christened, married and buried are an essential part of every genealogy tree and family album.

A series of easy-to-use CD Roms is planned for publication, and an increasing number of Frith photographs will be able to be viewed on specialist genealogy sites. A growing range of Frith books will be available on CD.

Frith Products

All Frith photographs are available Framed or just as Mounted Prints, and can be ordered from the address below. From time to time other products - Address Books, Calendars, Table Mats, etc - are available.

The Internet

Already thousands of Frith photographs can be viewed and purchased on the internet. By the end of the year 2000 some 60,000 Frith photographs will be available on the internet. The number of sites is constantly expanding, each focussing on different products and services from the Collection.

Some of the sites are listed below.

www.townpages.co.uk
www.icollector.com
www.barclaysquare.co.uk
www.cornwall-online.co.uk

For more detailed information on Frith companies and products, look at these sites:

www.francisfrith.co.uk
www.frithbook.co.uk
www.francisfrith.com

See the complete list of Frith Books at:

www.frithbook.co.uk

This web site is regularly updated with the latest list of publications from the Frith Book Company Ltd. If you wish to buy books relating to another part of the country that your local bookshop does not stock, you may purchase on-line.

For further information, trade, or author enquiries please contact us at the address below:
The Francis Frith Collection, Frith's Barn, Teffont, Salisbury, Wiltshire, England SP3 5QP.
Tel: +44 (0)1722 716 376 Fax: +44 (0)1722 716 881 Email: uksales@francisfrith.com

To receive your FREE Mounted Print

Mounted Print
Overall size 14 x 11 inches

Cut out this Voucher and return it with your remittance for £1.50 to cover postage and handling. Choose any photograph included in this book. Your SEPIA print will be A4 in size, and mounted in a cream mount with burgundy rule lines, overall size 14 x 11 inches.

Order additional Mounted Prints at HALF PRICE (only £7.49 each*)

If there are further pictures you would like to order, possibly as gifts for friends and family, acquire them at half price (no additional postage and handling required).

Have your Mounted Prints framed*

For an additional £14.95 per print you can have your chosen Mounted Print framed in an elegant polished wood and gilt moulding, overall size 16 x 13 inches (no additional postage and handling required).

---

* IMPORTANT!
These special prices are only available if ordered using the original voucher on this page (no copies permitted) and at the same time as your free Mounted Print, for delivery to the same address

---

Frith Collectors' Guild

From time to time we publish a magazine of news and stories about Frith photographs and further special offers of Frith products. If you would like 12 months FREE membership, please return this form.

Send completed forms to:
The Francis Frith Collection, Frith's Barn, Teffont, Salisbury, Wiltshire SP3 5QP

Voucher for FREE and Reduced Price Frith Prints

Picture no.	Page number	Qty	Mounted @ £7.49	Framed + £14.95	Total Cost
		1	**Free of charge***	£	£
			£7.49	£	£
			£7.49	£	£
			£7.49	£	£
			£7.49	£	£
			£7.49	£	£

Please allow 28 days for delivery	* Post & handling	£1.50
Book Title	**Total Order Cost**	**£**

Please do not photocopy this voucher. Only the original is valid, so please cut it out and return it to us.

I enclose a cheque / postal order for £ . . . . made payable to 'The Francis Frith Collection'
OR please debit my Mastercard / Visa / Switch / Amex card

Number . . . .

Expires . . . . Signature . . . .

Name Mr/Mrs/Ms . . . .

Address . . . .

. . . .

. . . .

. . . . Postcode . . . .

Daytime Tel No . . . .   Valid to 31/12/01

The Francis Frith Collectors' Guild

Please enrol me as a member for 12 months free of charge.

Name Mr/Mrs/Ms . . . .

Address . . . .

. . . .

. . . .

. . . . Postcode . . . .

Free Print - see overleaf

A CENTURY *of*
DURHAM

The Vice Chancellor of Durham University, Sir Yorman Christopherson (centre) with, left to right, Dr B.J. Mason, Lord Todd of Trumpington, Professor H. Orton and Dr Athelstan Spilhaus, who received honorary degrees at the University Congregation at Durham Castle in 1970.

A CENTURY of DURHAM

CHARLIE EMETT

WHSmith

First published in the United Kingdom in 2002 by
Sutton Publishing Limited exclusively for
WHSmith, Greenbridge Road, Swindon SN3 3LD

British Library Cataloguing in Publication Data
A catalogue record for this book is available from the British Library.

ISBN 0-7509-3111-6

Illustrations

Front endpaper: Intercity locomotive *Durham Cathedral* with the real thing beyond, 1993.
Back endpaper: Durham World Heritage Site, 2000.
Half title page: Hexham Morris dancers at the city's folk festival, 1986.
Title page: The Sanctuary Knocker, Durham Cathedral.

The electroplated statue of Lord Londonderry by Raffaelle Monti (1858) in Durham's Market Place. The 3rd Marquess of Londonderry was a prominent nineteenth-century entrepreneur in the county's coal industry. It took a blind man to point out that the horse was not perfect: it does not have a tongue.

Typeset in 11/14pt Photina and produced by Sutton Publishing Limited, Phoenix Mill, Thrupp, Stroud, Gloucestershire GL5 2BU. Printed and bound in England by J.H. Haynes & Co. Ltd, Sparkford.

Contents

CITY OF DURHAM

Foreword

By The Right Worshipful The Mayor of Durham
Councillor Miss Eileen Rochford

I would like to thank Mr Emett for taking the time to research and write *A Century of Durham*. Durham has seen many changes take place within the City, the most recent of which was the opening of the Millennium City Development which includes a theatre, a lifelong learning centre and many other facilities for various sectors of the community.

I am sure the reader will find this a most interesting book and I hope that it will encourage you to come to visit our City.

Introduction

Durham is a city steeped in antiquity. Much of its history is connected with St Cuthbert, whose body lies in the city's magnificent cathedral built to house it. Durham Cathedral has been justifiably acclaimed by Pevsner and countless others as one of the architectural wonders of Europe. Both the cathedral and the castle rise from an upland area girt by the River Wear and known locally as the Peninsular. This promontory was called 'Dunholm' or 'hill island' and from this the name Durham is derived.

By virtue of its naturally defensive geographical position, Durham was chosen by William the Conqueror rather than Newcastle, 14 miles further north, as a bulwark against the Scots and the centre of Norman administration in the north. In 1072, while King William I was in Durham, he ordered the castle to be rebuilt, and special attention was given to strengthening its most vulnerable northern side. So effective were the design and structure of the rebuilt castle that all known methods of attack by the Scots were frustrated and they never did capture it. The Norman Chapel is the oldest part of the present building.

As an additional defence against the Scots, King William I instituted a line of non-hereditary prince bishops who became rulers in both spiritual and temporal matters. They enjoyed full royal rights and privileges within the prince bishopric, having their own mint, exchequer, parliament, judiciary and army. The first of the prince bishops was Walcher of

South-west prospect of Durham, *c.* 1600.

The keep of Durham Castle, 1840.

Lorraine (1071–81). He was well intentioned but an incompetent leader, and he was murdered at Gateshead in 1081. William St Carileph, a much stronger bishop, followed Walcher; he and a succession of others lived like kings in their castles and palaces at Durham and Bishop Auckland. In return for their privileges the prince bishops had to maintain a fortified garrison and fighting unit. In 1346 Bishop Neville helped to defeat the Scottish army in the western suburb of Durham now known as Neville's Cross. At the battle of Flodden Field in 1513 the Bishop of Durham's army contributed to the defeat of the Scots.

During the sixteenth and seventeenth centuries the splendour of ecclesiastic Durham diminished, as did the supremacy of Church over city. King Henry VIII abolished the bishopric during the Reformation. At the same time the cathedral was stripped of its shrines, relics and other embellishments, and its dedication to St Cuthbert, but its bishop was allowed to remain.

Until the Reformation the city of Durham had been subservient to the bishop. When Henry VIII dissolved the abbey the prior was transformed into a dean and twelve monks became cathedral prebendaries or canons. This change meant that the city lost much of the trade associated with pilgrims, festivals and fairs.

The prince bishops were reinstated after the Reformation but not with their original powers. Then during the Commonwealth of the seventeenth century the bishopric was again abolished and the dean and chapter suppressed. Both were restored by Charles II, but the Church never regained its former power in the city.

However, ahead lay a century of prosperity during which elegant architecture transformed the landscape.

When indomitable traveller Celia Fiennes visted Durham in 1698 she commented favourably on its appearance: 'I must say of the whole Citty of Durham its the noblest, cleane and pleasant buildings, streets large, well pitched.'

The government of Durham City is special in having its origins in the Palatinate powers of the prince bishops. The fortified part of the city was governed in early times by the constable of the castle while the rest was the bishop's property and was governed by a bailiff appointed by him. By virtue of their quasi-regal powers, it was the bishops who granted the charters to the city. Bishop Pudsey granted the first in either 1179 or 1180; and all it gave was freedom from certain tolls.

The incorporation of the city dates from Bishop Pilkington's charter of 1565. In it, subject to the bishop's veto, powers to make regulations for the government of the city became the responsibility of an alderman and twenty-four burgesses, who, provided they behaved themselves, held office for as long as the bishop thought fit.

Bishop Matthew's charter of 1602 decreed that twelve of the trade guilds could select twenty-four common councillors while the bishop would continue to appoint a bailiff and collect the market tolls. It was in 1602 that a mayor of Durham was first mentioned. During the Commonwealth the see was dissolved and the corporation bought the bishop's former rights in the city for £200, but lost them at the Restoration. Between 1770 and 1780 a bailiff appointed by the bishop governed Durham City; and in 1870 Bishop Egerton granted its last charter, which remained in use until the Municipal Corporation Act of 1835.

Durham has long been associated with academia. As far back as the thirteenth century the monks of Durham were sending pupils to Oxford, where Durham Hall was established in the fourteenth century. In 1380 Bishop Hatfield provided a permanent endowment in Durham, undertaking to maintain four monastic students and eight

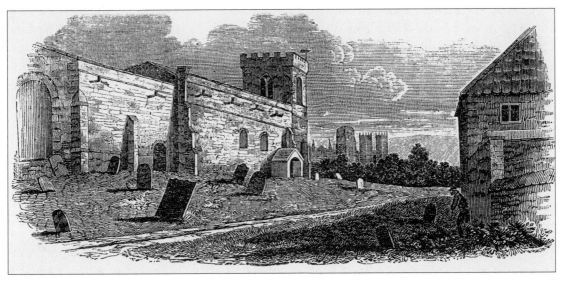

North-west view of St Giles's Church, 1840.

Great North Gate, Saddler Street, *c.* 1850.

secular ones, the monastery maintaining four monks. The present university was founded by an Act of Parliament in 1832, and its reputation was based largely on theological studies. Most of its graduates took Holy Orders in the Church of England. In Durham special emphasis has always been laid on the collegiate system. In 1837 Durham Castle became the home of the new-born university, whose part founder was William van Mildert, the last of the prince bishops.

Throughout its history Durham has remained a county town with little manufacturing industry, although it claims to have been the first producer of mustard in the world in 1720. During the eighteenth century four schemes to make the Wear navigable from Durham to its mouth and to cut a waterway to the Tyne had to be aborted: a new form of locomotion was imminent that would take over from the canals. The steam age had dawned and the steam engine, with its strong association with coal, would change the face of the region.

Although County Durham saw the birth of the railways and possessed the most productive coalfield in the country, Durham City remained largely unaffected by the expansion of the industrial age. Its main problems were a lack of level sites and water transport. Furthermore, the early railway entrepreneurs did not see commercial opportunities in expanding a rail network around the city. Durham found itself at a disadvantage compared with many other places in the area.

The focal point of Durham City is its Market Place which has medieval origins. It shares the Peninsular with Durham's cathedral and castle, and its most imposing features are the Guildhall, Town Hall, the church of St Nicholas and the statue of the 3rd Marquess of Londonderry. St Nicholas's Church, with its tall spire, dominates the eastern side of the Market Place. When it was built in 1858 by Darlington architect J.B. Pritchett it was described by the *Illustrated London News* as 'the most beautiful specimen of church architecture in the North of England'.

Two main streets, North and South Bailey, each a continuation of the other, run along the Peninsular parallel to the city wall for about half its length. Along them are found many houses of distinction, mostly with eighteenth-century frontages but with much older interiors. During the eighteenth and nineteenth centuries they were largely occupied by professional people.

Leading northwards from the Market Place is Claypath, a busy thoroughfare from which the River Wear can be seen in its horseshoe gorge, where it comes within 250 yards of making the Peninsular an island. The banks of the gorge, where the Wear is bridged six times, are perhaps the most beautiful parts of the magnificent city.

An imposing Victorian viaduct, which carries the East Coast main line, dominates the part of Durham beyond the Peninsular. After the cathedral, it is Durham's second largest structure.

Wharton Park, which was given to Durham City by Lloyd Wharton in the nineteenth century, contains a fine vantage point, Ruskin's View, from where the outlook northward is excellent. Nearby, half hidden by rolling parkland, is the Durham Light Infantry Museum which recounts the history of the DLI from 1758.

Among the many other delightful facets of Durham City to be found around the Peninsular are Kepier Hospital with its magnificent fourteenth-century gatehouse, and the

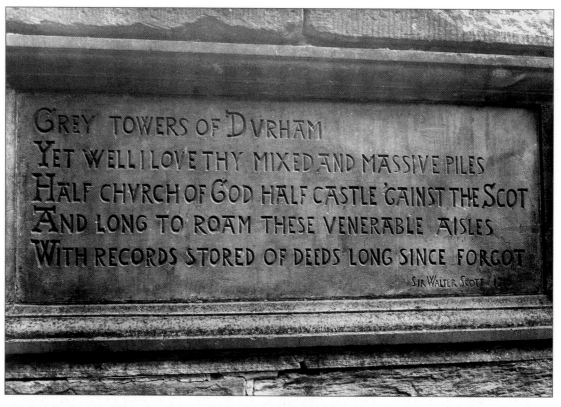

The fine view Sir Walter Scott saw of Durham Cathedral in 1810 inspired these lines, now chiselled into the parapet of Prebend's Bridge.

churches of St Giles and St Oswald. Then there are the seats of learning, the oldest and the one with the best view of the cathedral being St Mary's College.

Surrounding centres of learning are Grey's, St Aidan's, Van Mildert's and Collingwood Colleges, while three other features of note are in the university's extensive parkland; all are associated with the university. They are the Botanical Gardens in which is kept a special collection of sub-Alpine flora rescued from Teesdale Head when Cow Green Reservoir was built, the Museum of Oriental Art or Gulbenkian Museum – the only museum in the country entirely devoted to Eastern art and ornithology – and the university's observatory, designed by Salvin in 1841.

The city of Durham is famous for seven things,
Wood, Water and Pleasant Walks,
Law and Gospel,
Old Maids and Mustard.

Anon.

La Belle Epoque

The hundred years that dawned on 1 January 1900 would bring more change to Durham than any previous century. There would be tumult and conflict, but also excitement and achievement. To people like the lovers shown here strolling alongside the River Wear near the end of the nineteenth century, the future was enigmatic. Yet hope springs eternal in the human breast.

Judges of Assize, pictured here in about 1899 passing the former Ship Inn on Elvet Bridge, brought authority to the early days of the twentieth century. Elvet Bridge crosses the River Wear where it makes a right-angled turn to loop around the Peninsular. The bridge still has some of its original twelfth-century stonework. The waters swirled beneath it on 9 October 1903 when the Wear, in spate, rose to 13½ feet above its normal level.

Looking along Gilesgate from the Sherburn Road end, *c.* 1900. At this time horsepower was still mainly confined to horses and the motorcar had yet to make its mark. The large house on the left, The Mount, occupied the site of an old toll house. Gilesgate Methodist Chapel is the second building from the right.

At Durham University special emphasis has always been placed on the collegiate system. The students pictured here are its first women graduates, photographed in 1896. They all attended St Hild's.

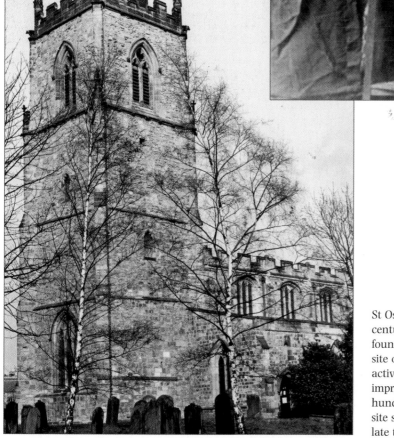

St Oswald's Church is dedicated to the seventh-century king and martyr who invited Aidan to found a missionary base on Lindisfarne. This is the site of the earliest known recorded Christian activity in Durham City. The church, with its impressive tower, has changed little over the past hundred years. There has been a church on the site since Saxon times but the present building is late twelfth century.

Durham's fire engine on Palace Green, 1903. This was the year when an ancient well was discovered in the north-west corner of the castle's courtyard and when Hugh Mackay began manufacturing carpets in Durham. Carpet manufacture in the city developed from cloth weaving, an enterprise originally established by the corporation in 1614. Following many failures, the lease for a carpet factory was obtained by Gilbert Henderson in 1814. The business thrived and in 1903 Henderson sold it to Crossley's of Halifax, who promptly closed it. Hugh Mackay restarted the business the same year and it remained in Watergate until 1980 when all production transferred to Mackay's new factory at Dragonville just outside the city centre.

Gilesgate Post Office and Savings Bank where two helpful ladies would serve you with tea while you posted your letters, *c.* 1890.

Below: This watercolour over pencil landscape by Alfred William Hunt RWS (1836–96), which was exhibited at the Royal Jubilee Exhibition Manchester in 1887, at the Artists' Memorial Exhibition Liverpool in 1897 and at the Burlington Fine Arts Club London in 1897 was owned by Humphrey Robert Esq in 1908. On 8 June 1936 the then owner, Mrs William Newall, put it up for auction at Christies where, as lot 56, it was bought by a Mr Barnard. He got a bargain: it cost him £60 18*s*. In it Elvet Bridge is beautifully portrayed, backed by the cathedral.

Beneath the cathedral's two great western towers, on the wooded river bank, stands Durham's famous fulling mill (left). It was once owned by the priors of Durham, but today it is the home of the university's Museum of Archaeology and houses relics of the region's Anglo-Saxon past. Historically the fulling mill was known as the Jesus Mill.

Cobbled Saddler Street leads from the south-east corner of the Market Place, passing the castle on the right, beyond which Owengate branches right and Saddler Street continues straight ahead to join North Bailey end on. This is a very early photograph, taken in about 1850 when the science was in its infancy.

Looking down Framwellgate, early twentieth century. Horse and trap still dominate the picture but the bicycle and the petrol engine are already making their presence felt.

Above: Their lodge banner held high, miners of the Ryhope Lodge prepare for the Durham Miners' Gala in 1908. Robert Richardson MP is directly beneath the X to the left of the banner.

This highly elaborate Victorian miners' banner was a source of much pride to West Thornley Lodge members. More than that, a banner was a rallying point and gave a lodge member a sense of belonging.

The Rose and Crown, 43 New Elvet, garlanded with decorative flags and streamers as the city celebrated the coronation of King George V, 23 June 1911. Flags and bunting were also hung out in the Market Place and a huge bonfire was lit on Gilesgate Moor. The Rose and Crown is no more.

In this fine nineteenth-century picture of Durham's northern aspect, as seen from the upper part of Claypath when it was still fields, the cathedral dominates the skyline.

Evening shadows fall and the cathedral (left) and castle (right) are silhouetted against a grey sky. This scene remained constant throughout the twentieth century, a symbol of stability in a sea of change.

The railway viaduct, designed by the North Eastern Railway architect T.E. Harrison, was built in 1857. The new railway station was opened the same year just to the north of the city centre. It replaced Durham's original railway station at Gilesgate. This picture shows how the viaduct looked in the years immediately prior to the First World War. In 1989 the viaduct, the second tallest structure in Durham, was cleaned, strengthened and waterproofed. Overhead masts were then added and the main line was electrified.

Dryburn House was the Victorian residence of William Lloyd Wharton, chairman of the North Eastern Railway company. It later became one of the homes of Colonel Cuthbert Vaux, chairman of Vaux Breweries. During the Second World War Dryburn House became an emergency hospital for British servicemen and German prisoners of war.

Dryburn House, sometimes called Dryburn Hall, is set within spacious grounds. The name derives from two possible sources. Dryburn House is set on a hill where Durham's gallows once stood and its name may be a corruption of London's more famous Tyburn. However, legend has it that following the hanging of a Jesuit priest, the local stream, or burn, dried up, never to flow again.

The beautiful gardens of Dryburn House, *c.* 1912. The gardens occupy the part of Aykley Heads where the city's gallows stood. Here people were hanged by the neck until they were dead for such crimes as murder, sheep and horse stealing, robbery, housebreaking, treason and witchcraft. During the reign of Elizabeth I anyone thought to be a gypsy was summarily hanged. In those days justice was indeed rough.

The original St Nicholas's Church was founded in 1133 and survived until 1857 when, weakened beyond repair after its chancel was demolished as part of a road widening scheme, it was pulled down. The part of the Market Place fronting the church was its churchyard. In pre-Reformation times the Corpus Christi procession started at the church; when weavers from nearby Walkergate, which meant the cloth worker's street, celebrated their patron saint, St Blaise, it was here that they did it; and civic leaders held their special services there. A new church, the present St Nicholas's, was built on the site of the original one and, thanks to an afterthought by the then vicar, its tower, which serves as the main entrance, was erected on the south wall like the original one. This picture was taken in about 1913.

The Durham Equitable and Industrial Co-operative Society's main branch occupied a very prominent site in Claypath near the Market Place, The 'Store', as it was usually called, is pictured here before the First World War. It touched every part of the lives of its members – food, furniture, insurance, holidays, weddings, funerals and education. The Co-op offered goods at fair prices with the promise of a share in the profits via the quarterly 'divi' (dividend). This Claypath store was demolished prior to the building of the Claypath underpass in the mid-1960s.

This evocative early morning scene of the cathedral's northern aspect from Framwellgate was taken in about 1914. A horse having a well-earned break from pulling its trap is eating from its nosebag.

Answering the Country's Need

The first Durham Light Infantry soldier to gain the Victoria Cross in the First World War was Private Thomas Kenny. The citation stated that his 'pluck, endurance and devotion to duty were beyond praise'. Speaking to an audience in his home village of South Wingate in March 1916, Kenny said, 'All I can say is that I did my duty in France to the best of my ability.'

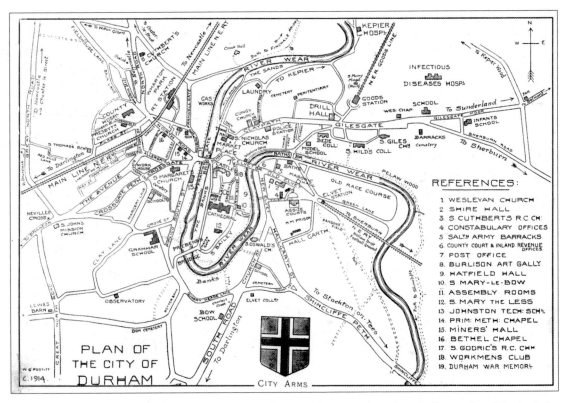

By 4 August 1914, when Britain declared war on Germany, the City of Durham had spread well beyond the confines of the Peninsular, as this contemporary plan by W.G. Footitt shows.

As far as local shopkeepers were concerned trade was as brisk in 1914 as it had been before hostilities. The horrors of war were distant.

In 1914 Durham folk were still habitually calling at the tea room near Prebends Bridge. It was once the home of Polish Count Joseph Borruwlawski, who was only 3 feet 3 inches tall. One of his many friends was Marie Antoinette who gave him a diamond ring. He visited England many times and fell in love with Durham, which he called 'my quiet place where my weary bones will rest'. He is buried in the cathedral.

This sketch by Eric Kennington RA is the embodiment of the Durham soldier during the First World War.

Presentations to local heroes in the Market Place, June 1917. Left to right: Private Richard Savage, 10th Royal Hussars (awarded the DCM in October 1914), Sergeant W.H. Smith MM, Durham Light Infantry, and Private M. Hanley, MM, Durham Light Infantry. In the centre is the Mayor, Frank W. Goodyear, and at the back on the right is the Very Revd Herbert Hensley Henson, at the time Dean of Durham, later Bishop.

DLI battle honours proudly displayed on the regiment's drums. Durham soldiers were present at all the crucial and most bloody battles of the First World War – Ypres, Arras, the Somme.

No more than a boy. Private Albert Richardson, 8th Durham Light Infantry, 1915. Albert was a bugler and served in France during the First World War. He returned from the Western Front and followed his father, Albert senior, into the post of head gardener at St Hild's College.

2nd Lieutenant Geraint Pasco Francis Thomas of the 2nd Durham Light Infantry. Son of Revd F. Thomas, Vicar of St Giles, Durham, he was attached to the Royal Flying Corps and was shot down over France in 1916. He spent the rest of the war as a prisoner.

The Victoria Cross is the rarest and most coveted British military decoration, awarded for outstanding gallantry. It was instituted by Queen Victoria in 1856. The bronze cross with the inscription 'For Valour' is suspended on the left breast from a crimson ribbon. It takes precedence over all other orders and medals. Since the medal's foundation only 1,351 Victoria Crosses have been awarded, eleven of them to soldiers of the Durham Light Infantry.

Captain Thomas de Courcy Hamilton won his VC while serving in the DLI in the Crimean War (1853–6), but VC awards are so rare that he deserves inclusion here. His citation says that when he led a small force against about thirty Russians he 'boldly charged the enemy thereby saving the works from falling into the hands of the enemy. He was conspicuous on the occasion for his gallantry and daring conduct.'

Sergeant John Murray also won his VC before the First World War at the Battle of Te Rango, fought on 21 July 1864 during the New Zealand Wars. Using his bayonet to good effect, he saved the life of John Byrne VC and gained the Victoria Cross for himself.

Roland Boys Bradford was a 2nd Lieutenant 2nd Battalion DLI when, in February 1915, he was awarded the newly created Military Cross 'for services rendered in connection with operations in the field', probably on the Western Front. On 1 October 1916, Bradford, now Lieutenant Colonel, won his Victoria Cross. The citation says: 'By his fearless energy under fire of all descriptions, and his skilful leadership of the two Battalions regardless of all danger, he succeeded in rallying the attack, captured and defended the objective and so secured the flank.'

Michael Wilson Heaviside of the DLI won his Victoria Cross at the Battle of Arras when, at about 2 o'clock on 6 May 1917, he risked almost certain death to rescue a wounded British soldier from a shell hole some 40 yards from a German brigade. The *London Gazette* announced the award on 8 June and the citation read that it was for his 'most conspicuous bravery and devotion to duty'.

On 12 July 1917 Major Louis Downey, acting Commanding Officer of the 13th Battalion DLI, wrote to the mother of one of his young officers: 'It is with very deep regret that I write to offer you my sincere sympathy . . . upon the death of your gallant son, Lieutenant Frederick Youens [pictured], who died of wounds on July 7th, 1917 . . . '. On 2 August the *London Gazette* announced the award of a posthumous Victoria Cross to 2nd Lieutenant Youens. The citation read: 'For most conspicuous bravery and devotion to duty.'

On 30 November 1917 German forces counter-attacked a push by the British Third Army on the Hindenburg Line. During the ensuing heavy fighting, Captain Arthur Moore Lascelles MC of 'A' Company, 14th (Services) Battalion, DLI, realising that the position his men were defending could be lost, led a charge that drove the enemy back, despite facing machine gun fire. On 11 January 1918 the *London Gazette* announced the award of the Victoria Cross to Captain Lascelles. The citation reads: 'The remarkable determination and gallantry of this officer . . . afforded an inspiration to all.' Later Arthur Lascelles said his men were the real heroes. 'It was due to the untiring devotion of a body of miners . . . that we were able to hold the ground. A more heroic company of men no officer could wish to command.'

Between the Wars

The Duke of Kent visits the Haig Homes, Sutherland Place, Sherburn Road, July 1937. The homes were built to house gravely disabled ex-soldiers and their families. While the Duke was there he admired the well-tended gardens and the panoramic views from the rear of the property.

With peace now a reality, people like those shown here during the 1920s in Old Durham gardens could relax a bit, take life a little easier.

Durham Golf Club, 1920s. After 1918 people wanted to forget about the war. Those who could afford it opted for a more relaxed lifestyle and self-indulgence became *de rigueur*. The jazz age had arrived and an American ragtime dance with much shaking of the hips and shoulders had taken England by storm. But for the most part, this was an evening pastime. During the day, weather permitting, golf was a big attraction. Some thrashed out business deals on a fairway so it was a game much involved with diplomacy. In 1924 a golf course planned by Lord Boyne was opened at Brancepeth near Durham City.

Many a demobbed squaddie found that strolling along the Wear on the Peninsular with a girl on his arm was far superior to the soul-destroying existence of the Western Front. If Durham could be said to have a 'monkey run', then this Peninsular walk, which passed the old fulling mill, was it.

By the 1920s a quarter of a million miners were employed in the north-east, and of these some 155,000 were employed in County Durham. In the main they originated from the countryside and the dales of County Durham and Northumberland, but some came from the city. Coalmining reached its peak in the area in 1923 when 170,000 were employed in County Durham. The part of Durham City covering the whole of the Peninsular had no mines because its seams were too narrow to be worked economically. But the miners' gala in the City was an annual rallying point for men from all British pits.

Here miners gathered behind their lodge banner proudly preparing to take their place in the Durham Miners' Gala big parade.

Ben Oliver looking at a likeness of his father, bottom left, on the Bewicke Main Lodge banner of *c.* 1924, the year Ramsay Macdonald (centre) became Prime Minister and Foreign Secretary of Britain's first Labour government.

Tudhoe Park Lodge banner of the National Union of Mineworkers was also carried in the 1924 Durham Miners' Gala parade.

As the situation on all British coalfields worsened during the spring and early summer of 1926 the *Northern Echo*'s Durham leadership began to absorb the latest news with more than a passing interest. Events were unfolding which could affect many of them personally; the way ahead was full of foreboding. The *Northern Echo*'s issue of 1 May carried the grim headline, 'No Settlement'. Events on Britain's coalfields had come to an impasse.

Sunderland District Tramways bus no. 56 in the Market Place, *c.* 1925. It is an AEC 2-tonner with coachwork by United. The Sunderland & District Omnibus Company was formed in 1927 to compete with Northern which subsequently took it over in 1931.

Little Hazel Davies sitting on the Blue Stone in St Giles's churchyard, 1932. The Blue Stone is thought to be a meteorite. It originally stood at the bottom of Gilesgate Bank next to the Dry Bridge. In 1923 it was taken to the churchyard for safe-keeping when the Dry Bridge was removed. It disappeared in the 1960s. This photograph was taken by Hazel's uncle, Foster Davies, who was churchwarden at St Giles.

In 1905 the first volume of the *Victoria County History of Durham* was published, followed in 1907 by volume two. The First World War delayed volume three, which came out in 1928. That year Durham Castle's seventeenth-century Senate Suite overmantel was repaired. There were splits in all three hand-carved panels, which had to be mended. The repairers did a commendable job.

During the 1930s much restoration work was done at Durham Castle. Outside the Great Hall the foundations were strengthened, while inside the floor of the Great Hall, pictured here, was completely rebuilt.

Restoring the castle wall stone by stone during the 1930s, before steel was used and before men wore hard hats.

During the 1930s the foundations of the west side of the castle were underpinned to stop them collapsing down the hillside.

During the depressed 1930s much of the country was feeling the draught. Walking their sheep to the auction mart, local farmers are backed by Durham Castle. Trade in those dark days was never very brisk.

Sheep clipping time at Hallgarth Farm near the Elvet area of Durham City, 1930s. There were no electric shears in those days and like so many other jobs around the farm, shearing was hard graft.

It was to a place behind the High Altar in Durham Cathedral that the body of St Cuthbert, in whose honour this great church was built, was brought on 29 August 1104, and for centuries thousands of pilgrims came to his shrine. In 1540 the shrine was destroyed by the King's Commissioners and St Cuthbert's body, still in its original coffin, was buried underneath where the shrine had stood. There it remained along with the head of St Oswald, King of Northumbria, who founded the see of Lindisfarne in 635. The wooden screen which separates the cathedral's Feretory from the Nine Altars transept was originally erected before 1700. It was removed during the alterations of the 1860s and restored in 1936, although only the central panels are original.

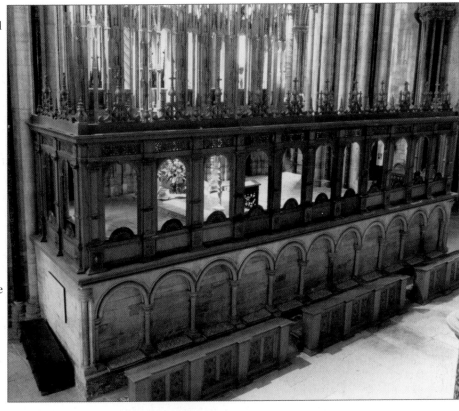

At least seven plans to bring a railway to Durham were abortive. One was opposed by the Senate of the university on the grounds that its proximity would be 'injurious to the morals of the students'. However, Durham's first station opened in 1844 on the northern side of Gilesgate and trains departing from it connected with the main London to Newcastle line at Belmont Junction. During the 1930s passengers were able to take holidays on the East Coast, enticed by London & North Eastern Railway posters like this one.

The Woolpack, 11 Framwellgate, 18 March 1933. On the previous day Denham Ringwood was murdered in the upstairs room. The Woolpack was a tenement property and was home to several families.

On 12 May 1937 the bells of the cathedral rang out in celebration of the crowning of King George VI. Two years later the direction to bell-ringers, shown here, had become, to all intents and purposes, obsolete. Now, the only time bell ringing was allowed was to warn of an invasion. It was 3 September 1939 and Britain was at war with Germany.

Durham Goes to War

In 1939 Alwynn Torrell Petre Williams was appointed the new Bishop of Durham. If the dream of Alwynn was for God to stop the war before it became unstoppable, he was to be disappointed. Already people were adjusting to new, wartime regulations. This car owner is ensuring that the beams of his headlights meet new government restrictions. Durham was more fortunate than many other cities: it was never bombed.

For the first time aerial warfare on a grand scale was a distinct possibility. Civilians faced the real fear of being bombed by the Luftwaffe. In an effort to minimise bombing casualties Anderson air raid shelters were supplied to householders throughout the land.

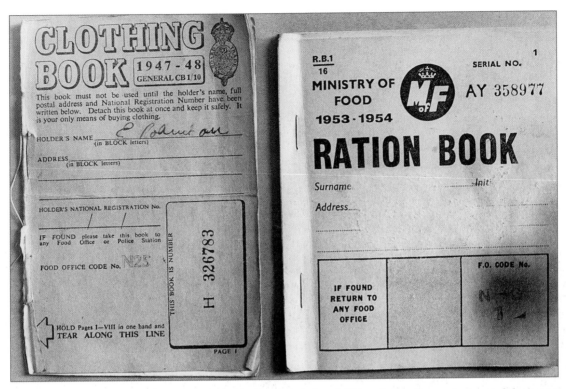

Clothing and ration books became part of everyday living for civilians during the war years and for many years after peace was declared.

Following the evacuation of the British Expeditionary Force from Dunkirk between 27 May and 3 June 1940, Britain found itself under siege. Its main lifeline – the North Atlantic convoys – was under severe pressure. This meant that the production of food had to be intensified at home, and so the Women's Land Army was formed. These are some Durham members of this wonderful organisation, which played an important part in the Allies' ultimate victory.

Government propaganda usually had a humorous slant to it, as this cartoon shows. Durham's flower gardens and lawns were transformed into kitchen gardens as the need to produce more food intensified. Digging for victory became *de rigueur*.

Unless you were in a reserved occupation like coalmining or farming or had failed a medical, you could expect to be called up soon after your eighteenth birthday. For many this was the first time they had been away from home for any length of time. Enlistment notices like this one fell through letterboxes all over Durham.

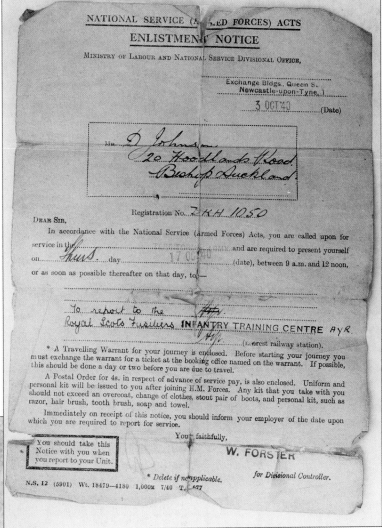

Some joined the Royal Navy. This young man became a signalman.

Flight Lieutenant James Nicholson joined the RAF, winning the Victoria Cross in 1940 when he was twenty-three years old. He shot down a German aircraft despite the fact that he was badly wounded and his aircraft was on fire. He parachuted to the ground where one of the Home Guard shot him in the buttocks. He recovered from his injuries but died in a crash in the Bay of Bengal in 1945.

Adam Wakenshaw joined the Army and served as a private in the DLI. On 11 September 1942 the *London Gazette* announced that he had been awarded a posthumous Victoria Cross for his 'conspicuous gallantry' and 'self-sacrifice and courageous devotion to duty'.

Breaking blackout regulations was a serious matter because at night any light could attract enemy aircraft, hence the production of humorous cartoons with a serious message.

Everywhere people were exhorted to 'make do and mend'. Mrs Sew-and-Sew's message was directed as much to Durham City as to the miners' villages spread across the county.

But there were compensations, one favourite being Vera Lynn, the forces' sweetheart, whose regular broadcasts linked troops with their loved ones. ENSA (Entertainment National Services Association) personnel entertained the forces in all theatres of war. From Durham to Dover, with bluebirds over its white cliffs immortalised by Vera Lynn, Britain's entertainment business made the war bearable. Without organisations like ENSA and the BBC and the artistes who made them tick, we could quite easily have lost the war.

On the home front, food and clothing coupons ensured that people got their fair share of what was available. In Durham shops, as elsewhere, there was still a reasonable supply of goods, and if the shopkeeper was a friend there was often a bit extra 'under the counter'.

The Ministry of Food pushed the sale of dried eggs, but on the black market real eggs – those with shells on – were available at a price. Spivs, the wide boys of the retail business who lived just outside the law, did a roaring trade.

On VE Day, 8 May 1945, the sky above the towers of Durham Cathedral cleared. *The Northern Echo* reported the German surrender.

Post-war Austerity
and the 1960s

The Durham Miners' Gala is deeply rooted in Socialism, so it came as no surprise when Labour Prime Minister Clement Attlee (left) and cabinet colleagues Hugh Dalton (inset) and Aneurin Bevan (right) joined Mr E. Moore, President of the Durham Miners' Association (centre), at the miners' gala in 1946.

It is 1949 and miners' gala participants are thronging Durham Market Place. This causes no traffic problems as there are no vehicles running along Silver Street towards the Market Place because of the gala, and the traffic control box (top left) is unmanned.

Nurses relaxing in the grounds of Aykley Heads, the new Preliminary Training School for nurses, 1949.

Excluding Miners' Gala Day, the traffic control box in the Market Place was always in use, as seen here in 1957. The famous traffic control box (also visible on the left of the picture on pages 68–9) was removed on 18 November 1975.

Miners' Gala Day 1950 and the old miner's expression of incomprehension echoes the question on the banner: why has our colliery closed? The colliery in question was at Hetton-le-Hole.

Miners and their families at a miners' gala *c*. 1950. The event was held on The Sands by the River Wear.

In 1952 the Durham Johnston School was moved from its original site at South Street to this new building at Crossgate Moor. In the same year Professor Allen's science 'B' building was built.

This picture, taken in June 1952, shows that miners' wives are just as capable of pulling a big crowd as their hubbies. Proudly carrying the banners of their respective sections, they put on a brave show. Moreover, they have a big advantage on their menfolk: they are better looking.

Arthur Michael Ramsey became the new Bishop of Durham in 1952. Pictured here at the cathedral's north door on 18 October of that year, he is seeking sanctuary, believing himself to be a sinner. The power of prayer being what it is, that should have done the trick; but when all is said and done, the bishop is human and subject to mortal frailty.

One warm, sunny June day in 1957 the banks of the Wear at Durham were lined with well-turned-out spectators, there to relax and cheer on their chosen crews at Durham's annual regatta.

Above: The spectators imagine that they are having the best of a glorious day. But we rowers are the ones who are having most of the fun. Ratty was right. There is *nothing* – absolutely nothing – half so much worth doing as simply messing about in boats.

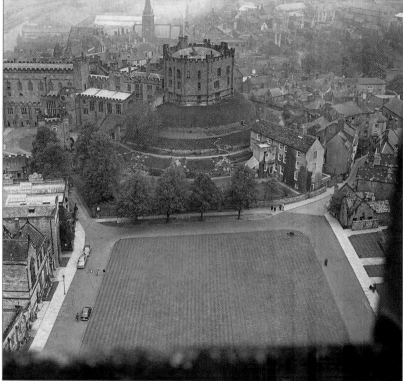

Durham Castle, seen here in 1959, the year the university's Grey College was founded, stands guardian over a city that never sleeps and is ever in a state of change.

Durham City Council was asked to provide free uniforms to safeguard the future of the mayor's bodyguard in 1960. Because of the cost of the ceremonial dress – frock coats and silk top hats – new recruits were not coming forward to join the 350-year-old organisation. It was founded in the 1600s and its members armed with pikes to accompany the mayor as he travelled the city collecting tolls. The bodyguard still exists with its ancient uniforms and pikes.

1960 was the year construction began on a new County Hall at Aykley Heads to the north of the city. It was also the year parts of Durham were flooded when the River Wear burst its banks.

Saddler Street in 1960, before the sixties began to swing, before traffic congestion and before many people were sucked into a more frenetic life style, epitomised by rock'n'roll groups like the Rolling Stones. Many of the problems that beset the twenty-first century have arisen because to get here we had to go through the 1960s.

The DLI Memorial Chapel in the cathedral, 1960. The well-tended silver candlesticks and the cross, the flags so proudly displayed overhead and the general air of love and concern bestowed upon this hallowed place speak volumes about those entrusted with its care.

University College students, 9 November 1961. Durham University is placed third, behind only Oxford and Cambridge, in the hierarchy of academia. It is number one in the north of England. University College is the oldest in Durham, founded in 1832.

Colleges come in all manner of architectural designs. St Chad's, seen here in 1961, blends in beautifully with its surroundings.

The Gulbenkian Museum of Oriental Art opened in 1961. It got off to a good start with a Buddhist Exhibition.

Durham County council in session in the County Hall, 27 February 1964. The new County Hall at Aykley Heads to the north of Durham City was opened by the Duke of Edinburgh in October 1963.

Durham's Shire Hall, seen here in 1962, is a handsome building and adds character to the city. It stands among many eighteenth-century buildings in Old Elvet, a wide street where horse fairs were once held. It is built of red brick, topped with a green copper dome. This imposing Victorian building was constructed in 1895 and extended in 1909. It was Durham's county hall until the new one opened at Aykley Heads in 1963. Since then the Shire Hall has been the administrative headquarters of Durham University. It was in the Shire Hall in 1909 that the first Labour county council in Britain assembled. Its first chairman was Peter Lee (1864–1935), a former miners' leader after whom the town of Peterlee is named.

The section of Durham around Sutton Street and Atherton Street had been earmarked to be cleared for a new road, some seven or eight years earlier than originally scheduled, when this picture was taken in January 1966. Angry Durham pensioners had been given premature notice to quit. The council works fast but not always in the interests of everybody. The clearance went ahead.

A pike-armed bodyguard, seen here on 29 July 1964, protects the mayor of Durham and the city's plate. The bodyguard is ten men strong but had only eight weapons in 1964: two pikes, two halberds, two lantern-carrier poles and two hefty staves. The mayor had just appealed for anyone with a spare, unwanted pike or halberd to get in touch with him! A pike-armed bodyguard still exists today.

St Aidan's College sits unobtrusively on a hill and has distinctive views of the cathedral. Built in 1961, it was designed by Sir Basil Spence who also designed a chapel for it, which was never built. Two residential wings half-embrace its semi-formal gardens which were designed by Brian Hackett. This is the college's airy, junior common room in 1964. St Aidan's was founded as a college for women but became co-educational in 1981.

Surrounded by gardens and woodland, St Hild's was a training college for women teachers when this picture was taken in 1965. Here enjoying a walk through the grounds, having just settled in, are (left to right), Ann Boyd, Ann Cooper, Celia Purdy, Jane Shute, Patricia Neale, Gillian Cauldwell, Joan Laverick, and Elizabeth Webster. They should be all right at St Hild's because next door was St Bede's College for men. The two have since merged.

Rowing crews preparing for the Head of the River race on the Wear, 1963.

Just before Christmas 1965 this lorry slowly made its way up the bank from Elvet Bridge. It was just one of a total of 6,400 vehicles using Durham's roads in a day. A traffic census showed that of these vehicles thirty-three were articulated lorries with trailers and thirty-eight had three or more axles. They were among 680 commercial vehicles other than light vans. At an inquest following a road death in Durham, the coroner, Mr Lance Bacon, appealed to drivers of heavy lorries to avoid the narrow streets and steep hills of Durham when making through journeys.

Secretary of State for Employment Barbara Castle on the balcony of the County Hotel with her hand to her ear, 20 July 1968. She and Prime Minister Harold Wilson were in the city to watch the Durham Miners' Gala. The fate of the gala, once regarded as Britain's greatest trade union and political rally, is currently being decided by miners' leaders.

In 1967 Dunelm House, University of Durham, won a Royal Institute of British Architects award for Northern England (Region One). Architects' Co-Partnership of London were responsible for the building's design.

Museum Square was one of the most historic of the city's squares, yet one of the least known. It had nestled in the shadow of Durham Cathedral, midway between Palace Green and the North Bailey, since the fourteenth century, but in 1968 it was to be demolished to make way for a new £200,000 university students' hostel.

The Seventies:
An Unusual Decade

Cosin's Hall, overlooking Palace Green, and other nearby properties were said to be in a very dangerous state of repair in 1972. The university planned to rebuild all the rooms behind the splendid façade which still remains. It dates from the seventeenth century and is full of charm. Perhaps the architects were inspired by Bruges.

Durham has had its fair share of students with divergent views. Such individuals are usually tolerated by a benign populace, even the student in this 1971 picture with a supercilious look on his face.

Earl's House Hospital, 1970. The building is architecturally light and airy, which is what is expected of a modern hospital, but will it stand the test of time?

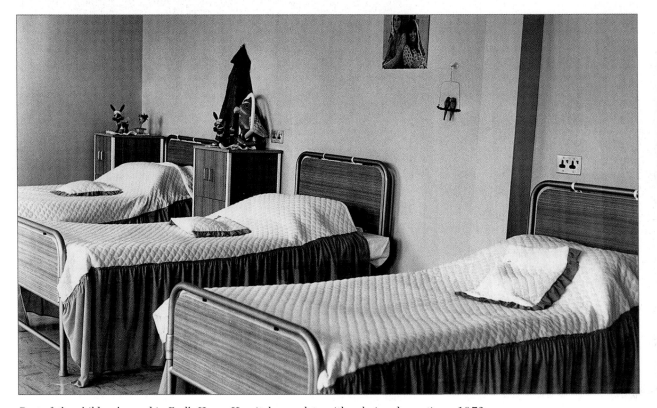

Part of the children's ward in Earl's House Hospital, complete with calming decorations, 1972.

Newcastle fans claim that theirs is the greatest team in the north-east, a claim disputed by Sunderland and Middlesbrough supporters, among others. However, there is no doubt about Durham's proud boast that it has the largest football cup in the world! It is the Lahore Trades Football Challenge Cup, pictured here in 1971. Durham won it in India in 1929 and it is kept in the DLI Museum.

In 1972 another bridge was constructed across the River Wear at Durham. It was a footbridge and still spans the river at Maiden Castle.

The city once had a generous quantity of public houses but many have now gone. The Market Tavern, seen here in 1975, is the only one remaining in the Market Place.

Saddler Street was experiencing ever-growing traffic problems in 1973. But all was not lost. The vehicles were moving almost as fast as they did before the petrol engine was invented.

Traffic restrictions were in force at Elvet Bridge by June 1975.

Archaeological dig leader John Clipson inspects some clay pipes excavated from Kiln Bank, Silver Street, November 1975.

Sledgers and a skier were quick to take advantage of winter snowfalls in January 1976. The city's hilly open spaces provide good conditions for winter sports.

Of course 1976 was a strange year for weather. After January's snow came one of the hottest summers on record but by October the Wear was in spate.

In the 1720s a group of entrepreneurs, including prominent local landlord John Bowes, hoped to make Durham a sea port. As a token of their intent John Bowes presented Durham with a statue of Neptune, the god of the sea. The project failed but the statue remained in the Market Place. In 1923, due to increased traffic, Neptune was re-erected in Wharton Park, where he remained when this picture was taken in 1978.

During the 1970s pop festivals were the rage throughout Britain. The venue for this event on 20 June 1976 was The Sands alongside the River Wear, a location more usually associated with the Durham Miners' Gala.

In a large edifice like Durham Cathedral many of the people who see to its smooth running are volunteers like thirteen-year-old Alex McAtear, seen here in September 1978. Alex was a cathedral guide.

There is more to Durham Cathedral than meets the eye. There certainly seemed to be a lot of activity and puzzlement in its undercroft in 1978. The lady at bottom right has found something unholy and nobody seems to know what it is.

In 1978 Bovis Property Division's Milburngate Centre, a £1.6 million retail and office development, was opened close to Framwellgate Bridge. The name Milburngate is derived from a burn that ran down the North Road valley and drove two mills, one on the site of the bus station and the other, the Clock Mill, near the river.

The Durham Light Infantry Museum and Art Gallery is set within the parkland of Aykley Heads Estate. Its exhibitions tell the story of the DLI from its birth in 1758 to its last parade past the cathedral in 1968. The original DLI Museum opened just after the First World War in Newcastle. In 1939 the regiment moved to Brancepeth Castle and the museum moved with it. In the 1960s the new museum was built on the site of Durham City's last working colliery. It opened in 1969 and is pictured here in 1978.

In about 1930 the Bishop of Durham purchased some land between Station Approach and Framwellgate to protect the view. It was to no avail: Durham City Council compulsorily purchased the land in 1979. The land remained open until 2001 and is currently under development for private housing.

The thermodynamics laboratory at the university's Department of Engineering, 1979.

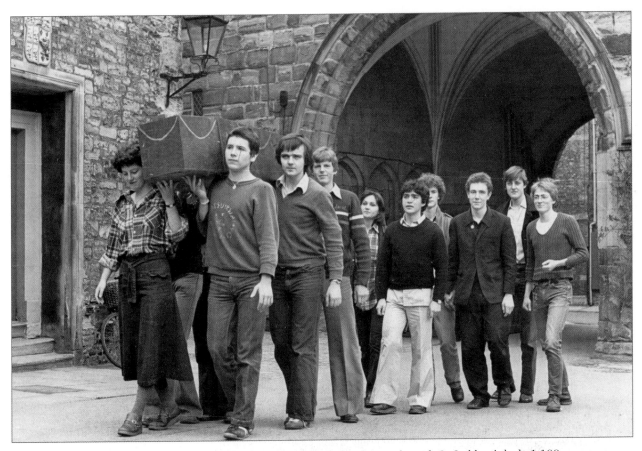

Students taking part in a charity event in 1978 retrace the steps taken by monks with St Cuthbert's body 1,100 years ago.

A single rose, a tribute to 12,000 fallen soldiers of the First World War, was brought to England from Belgium after Ypres, one of the bloodiest battles of the First World War. Sixty-two years later in 1978 a piece of the rose was planted in the grounds of the cathedral. At the moving ceremony DLI buglers sounded the last post.

Above: In 1979 the cathedral's bells had to be moved to make way for alterations to the tower. Maintenance man George Scott is working among the bells, which are tied to prevent ear splitting rings. One can imagine Mr Scott calling at his local, pointing to the whisky and asking for 'the Bells, the Bells'.

Not all Durham's buildings live out their lives fulfilling the uses for which they were originally built. In November 1978 the church of St Mary-le-Bow was re-opened by the Bow Trust as The Durham Heritage Centre.

St Godric's Convent, Castle Chare, Durham, in 1979 before it was renovated and converted to the Castle Chare Community Centre.

Of the three streets leading from Durham Market Place, a short one leads north to Leazes Road, one goes east and one goes south-west, descending to Framwellgate Bridge. This is Silver Street in 1978. One of the wealthiest citizens of Durham, John Duck, had his home in Silver Street. He arrived in Durham in 1655 intent on becoming a butcher's apprentice but because he did not know where he had been born, no butcher would employ him. Legend has it that one day as he walked, disheartened, by the Wear a raven dropped a gold coin at his feet. From this coin John Duck made his fortune, becoming a cattle dealer. In 1680 he became mayor of Durham. He was later made a baronet, becoming Sir John Duck of Haswell on the Hill.

East from the Market Place is Saddler Street, seen here in 1979. On it is The House of Andrews, which has a teapot prominently displayed outside. Today this is a wine shop.

Towards the Millennium and Beyond

Father Francis Rice inspects organ repair work at St Godric's Roman Catholic Church, 1987.

Ray Pallister, tutor in charge, Nevilles Cross College, gets to grips with the latest in computer technology in 1986!

Eunice Jenvey with a collection of Count Joseph Borruwlawski's clothing, 1985. Only 3 feet 3 inches tall, the Polish count travelled widely across Europe and had a particular love of Durham which he called his 'quiet place'.

Students at Durham Regatta, 1986.

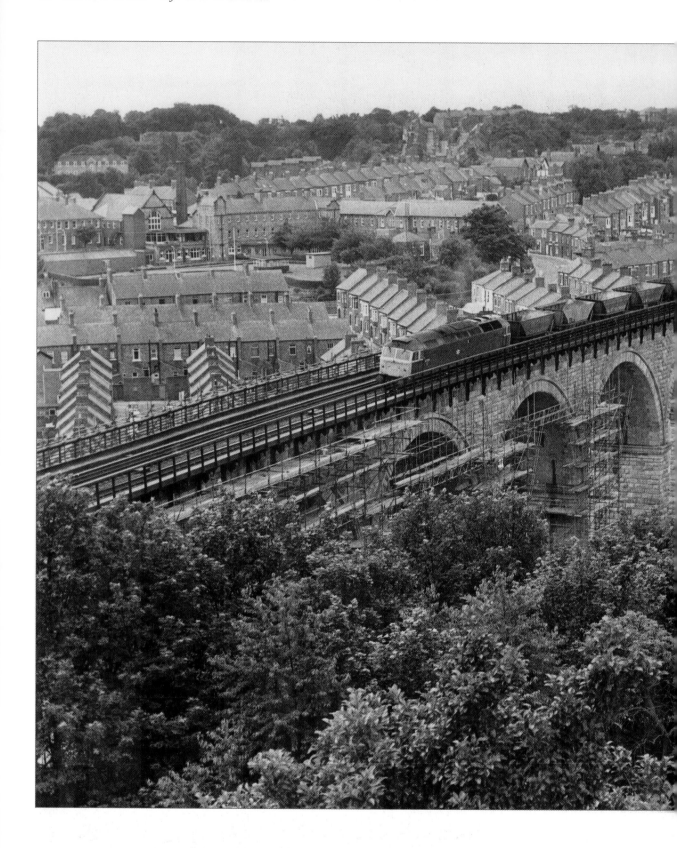

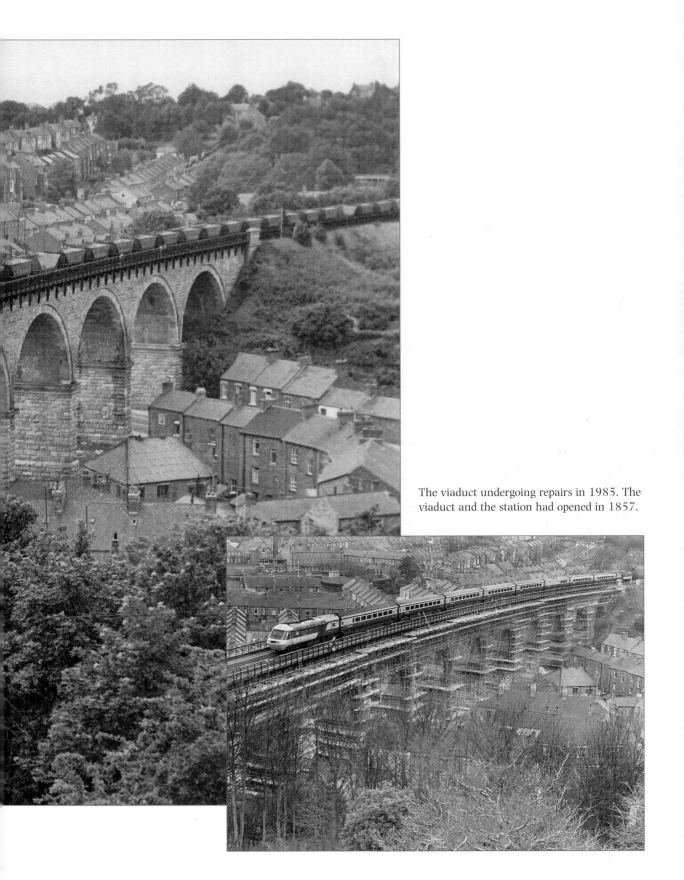

The viaduct undergoing repairs in 1985. The viaduct and the station had opened in 1857.

In 1987 Durham Cathedral and Castle were declared a World Heritage Site, one of only a few in the country selected for this distinction by the United Nations Educational, Scientific and Cultural Organisation (UNESCO). Left is the cathedral's Galilee Chapel; the cloisters are below.

In 1989 Durham teachers held an art exhibition. Sue Harford proudly displays her painting while keeping a tight hold of her model, the *Northern Echo*.

Honorary graduates – left to right Professor Gordon Stone, Hans Dietrich Genscher, Sir Peter Ustinov and Lady Barbirolli – receiving their degrees at Durham Castle on 30 June 1993.

119

What joy it is gliding along the River Wear, surrounded by such beauty. The Thames does not hold a monopoly on liquid history. This picture was taken in 1993.

1993 was the 900th anniversary of Durham Cathedral and the Post Office issued a special first-day cover, held here by Cliff Garside, to commemorate this special birthday.

Left to right: Norman Richardson, John Martin and Maurice Crinthorne proudly display an award for Kingsgate footbridge, seen behind them, in 1993.

Another year, another award. This time it is a Railway Heritage Trust award for the railway station. This picture was taken in 1994, the year Michael Turnbull became the new Bishop of Durham.

There is something a little bit special about shopping in the friendly atmosphere of Durham's indoor market. Stallholders like Marion Dale – seen here in 1994 talking to the market's new business manager, Eileen Watkins – don't just sell their products, they take a genuine interest in their customers and consequently barriers are broken down and friendships are forged. This is the civilised way to shop.

Any Durham University professor will tell you that the word castle is derived from the Latin *castellum*, the diminutive of which is *castrum*, meaning fort. The Normans built a great eastern rampart at the north end of the Peninsular on which the cathedral stands, it being the only stretch of 'Dun Holm' not encircled and protected by the River Wear. In 1072, when William I visited Durham, he ordered the castle to be rebuilt as a defence against the Scots. Until 1836 the castle was the palace of the prince bishops. It is now home to University College, the foundation college of England's third oldest university. It houses one of the finest Romanesque palaces in England. Its senior common room, in which a smiling Vivien Bollon is pictured here in 1994, is a far cry from how it looked when the castle was first built.

Work began on the construction of Durham Cathedral in 1093, authorised by the Prince Bishop William St Carileph. The cathedral celebrated its 900th birthday in 1993, but the city is ninety-eight years older. In the summer of 995 monks carrying the coffin of St Cuthbert established a settlement at 'Dun Holm' that was to become their saint's final resting place. The monks later became known as the Cuthbert Community. In the summer of 1995 the city celebrated its 1,000th birthday. A millennium celebration was held at which monks of the Cuthbert Community played an important part. This was followed by Holy Communion in the cathedral.

Above: Durham's streets are no longer filled to overflowing during the miners' gala. No longer do the pitmen walk behind their individual lodge banners as once they did. As this turn of the century picture shows the miners are fewer, the banners more spread out. For so many of the mining community who were regularly part of this huge parade the future may be uncertain; but for all of them, there is nothing uncertain about their pride in belonging to an unglamorous but essential industry that has served this country so well for so long.

Most things are transitory, prince bishops and miners among them; but Durham's greatest assets, its university and its cathedral, represent eternal truths. This picture of the cathedral's High Altar shows the Neville screen, behind which St Cuthbert's body lies. Prominent above the altar is the magnificent rose window which has drawn the eye and aspirations of millions of believers over centuries. From this holy place at the very heart of Durham comes hope for the future not only of Durham, but of the whole world.

Acknowledgements and Picture Credits

To David Kelly, managing director of the *Northern Echo* and to Peter Barron, editor of this great newspaper, go my very special thanks for allowing me to explore the *Echo*'s picture library, always a most enjoyable and informative occupation. All the images in the book belong to the *Northern Echo*. Thanks also to Christine Watson and Jane Whitfield, two intelligent ladies whose great charm is only surpassed by their beauty. They guard the *Echo* archives and make yummy coffee. Bless you both! To the Worshipful the Mayor of Durham, Councillor Eileen Rochford, sincere thanks for your co-operation in this venture. Many thanks to Stephen Shannon of the Durham Light Infantry Museum and Art Gallery for permission to quote from your inspiring book about Durham's VCs, *Beyond Praise*. Your contribution to the book has been of great value and I thank you for your help. For your valued help, thank you BEAMISH, North of England open air museum. My thanks also to Gillian Lovett of the City of Durham Council, Claire Gardiner of the Public Relations Office at the University of Durham and Anne Hall from the DLI Museum and Art Gallery. Eagle Graphics, I salute you for converting my scrawl into good type. As ever, the editorial side is in the safe hands of a brilliant team at Sutton Publishing, headed by Senior Commissioning Editor Simon Fletcher. Many thanks to you, Simon, and to Commissioning Editor Sarah Moore, Publishing Coordinator Joyce Percival, and Assistant Editor Michelle Tilling. What a super team you are and what a pleasure it is working with such lovely friends! We're a great team. Something must be my responsibility. Ah, yes, the errors: they are all mine.